cook & enjoy

Chicken

cook & enjoy

Chicken

Delicious recipes for the everyday cook

This edition published by Parragon Books Ltd in 2016

LOVE FOOD is an imprint of Parragon Books Ltd

Parragon Books Ltd
Chartist House
15–17 Trim Street
Bath BA1 1HA, UK
www.parragon.com/lovefood

ISBN 978-1-4748-4399-7
Printed in China

Cover photography by Charlie Richards
Cover home economy by Mima Sinclair
Introduction by Linda Doeser

Notes for the Reader
This book uses both metric and imperial measurements. Follow the same units of measurement throughout; do not mix metric and imperial. All spoon measurements are level: teaspoons are assumed to be 5 ml, and tablespoons are assumed to be 15 ml. Unless otherwise stated, milk is assumed to be full fat, eggs and individual vegetables are medium, pepper is freshly ground black pepper and salt is table salt. Unless otherwise stated, all root vegetables should be peeled prior to using.

The times given are an approximate guide only. Preparation times differ according to the techniques used by different people and the cooking times may also vary from those given.

For best results, use a food thermometer when cooking meat. Check the latest government guidelines for current advice.

Cover image shows the Cajun Chicken Salad on page 62.

contents

Introduction

Chicken is a popular favourite with adults and children alike, perhaps because it is such a versatile ingredient that there are heaps of different dishes to suit all tastes. It can be prepared in lots of ways, ranging from classic roasts to speedy stir-fries and from spicy curries to rich and satisfying stews. It makes great sandwiches, wraps, salads, soups and kebabs and is the perfect partner for pasta and rice. It is perfect for any occasion, from an elegant dinner party with friends to a relaxed family barbecue.

The delicate flavour of chicken combines well with many kinds of other ingredients and cooks in every corner of the world have created their own unique repertoire of chicken dishes. Ginger, soy sauce, noodles, lemon grass, chillies and fresh coriander feature in Asian dishes, while olives, wine, garlic, tomatoes and ham characterize Mediterranean recipes.

A subtle use of herbs and spices brings out the full flavour of chicken. Tarragon, with its slight hint of aniseed, and basil work particularly well. Piquant hot spices are typical of Mexican, Caribbean and Indian cuisines, and warm aromatic spices feature in Middle Eastern and Cajun dishes. Common accompaniments to chicken include honey, sherry, prawns, fruit (especially citrus fruit), cheese, mushrooms and all kinds of vegetables.

Not only is chicken a versatile ingredient, it can also have health benefits. Chicken is an excellent source of protein, B vitamins and minerals, and is naturally low in fat, making it an ideal ingredient if you are watching your weight. If low fat is your focus, it is important to remove the skin before cooking and eating chicken, as this is where the fat is. The B vitamins that chicken contains are important in our diet as they help release energy from our food into our bodies.

buying, storing & preparing chicken

When choosing a fresh chicken look for one with a plump breast and creamy-coloured skin. The tip of the breast bone should be pliable. These days chicken is almost always sold oven-ready (that is, plucked and cleaned), although the giblets – heart, liver, neck and gizzard – may be included, particularly with frozen birds.

The smallest birds are four- to six-week-old poussins, which weigh 450–550 g/1–1 lb 4 oz and make a perfect serving for one. Double poussins are eight to ten weeks old, weigh 800–900 g/1 lb 12 oz–2 lb and will serve two people. Three-month-old spring chickens, ideal for three to four people, weigh 1–1.25 kg/2 lb 4 oz–2 lb 12 oz, while roasters are twice this age and weigh 1.5–2 kg/3 lb 5 oz–4 lb 8 oz. Boiling fowl, which make superb soups and good stews as long as they are cooked gently for 2–3 hours, are usually about a year old and weigh 2–3 kg/ 4 lb 8 oz–6 lb 8 oz. Corn-fed chickens are an attractive yellow colour and are about the same size as roasters. As they are usually free-range and often organically raised rather than intensively reared, they tend to be a little more expensive.

A wide variety of chicken pieces are available. It is often more economical to buy a whole bird and cut it into serving pieces yourself, but ready-prepared pieces are very convenient. The leg consists of drumstick and thigh meat and is a good choice for casseroles and stews. Drumsticks are great for frying and a popular choice for barbecues. Thighs are also good for slow cooking methods and skinless boneless thighs are ideal for stuffing. Chicken breasts have a milder flavour than the dark meat and are good for stuffing, stir-frying or pan-frying in butter. While chicken wings don't have much meat, they make popular nibbles at barbecues or pan-fried as a starter. Diced and minced chicken pieces are also widely available, although it is easy to prepare these at home using skinless, boneless chicken breasts.

Store frozen birds in the freezer and thaw them completely before cooking. To do this, open one end of the bag and leave the chicken to thaw in a cool place for up to 12 hours. Smaller birds, such as poussins, will take less time. Remove the giblets, if there are any, as soon as you can. The chicken is ready for cooking when the legs are soft and flexible and there are no ice crystals in the cavity. You can speed up the process slightly by putting the bird, in the sealed bag, in a bowl of cold water.

Do not try to thaw frozen chicken in hot water. Store fresh birds on a plate, loosely covered with greaseproof paper or clingfilm on the bottom shelf of the refrigerator. Cook within three days of purchase.

Raw chicken may contain salmonella and other bacteria that can cause food poisoning so always wash the chopping board, knives and other utensils thoroughly after preparing it. Ideally, keep a specific chopping board for poultry that is dishwasher safe so it can withstand high temperatures. Wash your hands both before and after handling raw chicken and before touching any other ingredients. Do not rinse the chicken under cold running water. Although this may seem like a sensible precaution, it's more likely to spread bacteria, not only over the chicken but also all over you and the kitchen, than to get rid of them.

When cooking chicken on a barbecue, make sure that you do not use the forks, knives, tongs and so on for other ingredients after you have used them for chicken, unless the utensils have been thoroughly washed in hot soapy water first.

Thorough cooking destroys the bacteria and it is very important that chicken is cooked all the way through before serving. Test this by inserting the point of a sharp knife in the thickest part of the meat. If the juices run clear, then it is ready. If there are any traces of pink, cook for a few minutes more and test again. Check too that the

base of the cut is firm and white. The thickest part on a whole bird is the inside of the thigh.

If you're planning to stuff a chicken for roasting, do so just before putting it into the oven. Pack the stuffing loosely and remember to weigh the chicken afterwards so you can calculate the cooking time. Any leftover stuffing may be cooked separately. Don't stuff the body cavity of a large bird as it may not cook all the way through. Allow 20 minutes per 450 g/1 lb, plus 20 minutes extra at 200°C/400°F/Gas Mark 6 in a preheated oven. When the chicken is cooked through, remove it from the oven, cover with foil and leave to rest for 10–15 minutes before carving.

chicken stock

makes about 2.5 litres/4½ pints

1.3 kg/3 lb chicken wings and necks

2 onions, cut into wedges

4 litres/7 pints water

2 carrots, roughly chopped

2 celery sticks, roughly chopped

10 fresh parsley sprigs

4 fresh thyme sprigs

2 bay leaves

10 black peppercorns

STEP 1. Put the chicken wings and necks and the onions into a large saucepan and cook over a low heat, stirring frequently, until lightly browned.

STEP 2. Add the water and stir well to scrape all the sediment from the base of the pan. Gradually bring to the boil, skimming off the foam that rises to the surface. Add all the remaining ingredients, partially cover and simmer for 3 hours.

STEP 3. Strain the stock into a bowl, leave to cool, cover and store in the refrigerator. When cold, discard the layer of fat from the surface. Use immediately or freeze for up to 6 months.

mole sauce

serves 6–10

9 mixed chillies, soaked in hot water for 30 minutes and drained

1 onion, sliced

2–3 garlic cloves, crushed

85 g/3 oz sesame seeds

85 g/3 oz toasted flaked almonds

1 tsp ground coriander

4 cloves

½ tsp pepper

2–3 tbsp sunflower oil

300 ml/10 fl oz chicken stock or vegetable stock

450 g/1 lb ripe tomatoes, peeled and chopped

2 tsp ground cinnamon

55 g/2 oz raisins

140 g/5 oz pumpkin seeds

55 g/2 oz plain chocolate, broken into pieces

1 tbsp red wine vinegar

STEP 1. Put the chillies into a food processor with the onion, garlic, sesame seeds, almonds, coriander, cloves and pepper and process to a thick paste.

STEP 2. Heat the oil in a saucepan, add the paste, and fry for 5 minutes. Add the stock with the tomatoes, cinnamon, raisins and pumpkin seeds.

STEP 3. Bring to the boil, reduce the heat and simmer, stirring occasionally, for 15 minutes. Add the chocolate and vinegar to the sauce. Cook gently for 5 minutes before using.

starters, soups & salads

chicken liver pâté

Serves 4

Difficulty: Medium

Prep: 25 mins, plus chilling
Cook: 15–20 mins

INGREDIENTS

140 g/5 oz butter

1 onion, finely chopped

1 garlic clove, finely chopped

250 g/9 oz chicken livers

½ tsp Dijon mustard

2 tbsp brandy (optional)

brown toast fingers, to serve

salt and pepper

CLARIFIED BUTTER (OPTIONAL)

115 g/4 oz lightly salted
 butter

STEP 1. Melt half the butter in a large frying pan over a medium heat, add the onion and cook for 3–4 minutes until soft and transparent. Add the garlic and cook for a further 2 minutes.

STEP 2. Check the chicken livers and remove any discoloured parts using a pair of scissors. Add the livers to the pan and cook over a medium-high heat for 5–6 minutes until brown.

STEP 3. Season well with salt and pepper and add the mustard and brandy, if using.

STEP 4. Process the pâté in a blender or food processor until smooth. Add the remaining butter cut into small pieces and process again until creamy.

STEP 5. Press the pâté into a serving dish or four small ramekins, smooth the surface and cover with clingfilm. If the pâté is to be kept for more than 2 days, you could cover the surface with a little clarified butter. Put the butter into a clean saucepan and heat until melted, then continue to cook for a few seconds until it stops bubbling. Leave the sediment to settle and carefully pour the clarified butter over the pâté.

STEP 6. Chill in the refrigerator until ready to serve, accompanied by toast fingers.

chicken balls with dipping sauce

Serves 4

Difficulty: Medium

Prep: 20 mins
Cook: 10–15 mins

INGREDIENTS

3 tbsp vegetable oil

2 large skinless, boneless
chicken breasts, cut into
2-cm/¾-inch pieces

2 shallots, finely chopped

½ celery stick,
finely chopped

1 garlic clove, crushed

2 tbsp light soy sauce

1 small egg

salt and pepper

6 spring onions, trimmed,
to serve

DIPPING SAUCE

3 tbsp dark soy sauce

1 tbsp rice wine

1 tsp sesame seeds

STEP 1. Heat half the oil in a frying pan over a high heat, add the chicken and stir-fry for 2–3 minutes until golden. Remove from the pan and set aside. Add the shallots, celery and garlic to the pan and stir-fry for 1–2 minutes until soft.

STEP 2. Put the chicken, shallots, celery and garlic into a food processor and process until finely minced. Add 1 tablespoon of the light soy sauce and just enough egg to process to a fairly firm mixture. Season to taste with salt and pepper.

STEP 3. Make the dipping sauce by mixing together the dark soy sauce, rice wine and sesame seeds in a small serving bowl and set aside.

STEP 4. Shape the chicken mixture into 16–18 walnut-sized balls. Heat the remaining oil in a frying pan or wok, add the chicken balls in small batches and stir-fry for 4–5 minutes until golden brown. As each batch is cooked drain on kitchen paper and keep hot.

STEP 5. Add the spring onions to the pan and stir-fry for 1–2 minutes until they begin to soften, then stir in the remaining light soy sauce. Serve with the stir-fried spring onions and the bowl of dipping sauce.

chicken satay skewers with peanut sauce

Serves 4

Difficulty: Medium

Prep: 30 mins, plus 2 hours marinating
Cook: 15–20 mins

INGREDIENTS

450 g/1 lb boneless chicken
breasts, cut into 2-cm/
¾-inch cubes

4 tbsp soy sauce

1 tbsp cornflour

2 garlic cloves,
finely chopped

2.5-cm/1-inch piece fresh
ginger, peeled and
finely chopped

roughly chopped cucumber,
to serve

PEANUT SAUCE

2 tbsp groundnut oil or
vegetable oil

½ onion, finely chopped

1 garlic clove, finely chopped

4 tbsp crunchy peanut butter

4–5 tbsp water

½ tsp chilli powder

STEP 1. Put the chicken cubes into a shallow dish. Mix the soy sauce, cornflour, garlic and ginger together in a small bowl and pour over the chicken. Cover and leave to marinate in the refrigerator for at least 2 hours.

STEP 2. Meanwhile, soak 12 bamboo skewers in cold water for at least 30 minutes. Preheat the grill and thread the chicken pieces onto the skewers. Place the skewers in a grill pan and cook under the preheated grill for 3–4 minutes. Turn and cook for a further 3–4 minutes, or until cooked through.

STEP 3. Meanwhile, to make the sauce, heat the oil in a saucepan, add the onion and garlic and cook over a medium heat, stirring frequently, for 3–4 minutes until soft. Add the peanut butter, water and chilli powder and simmer for 2–3 minutes until thickened. Serve the skewers immediately with the warm sauce and cucumber.

sticky ginger & soy chicken wings

Serves 4

Difficulty: Easy

Prep: 15 mins, plus marinating
Cook: 12–15 mins

INGREDIENTS

12 chicken wings

2 garlic cloves, crushed

2.5-cm/1-inch piece fresh ginger

2 tbsp dark soy sauce

2 tbsp lime juice

1 tbsp clear honey

1 tsp chilli sauce

2 tsp sesame oil

lime wedges, to serve

STEP 1. Tuck the pointed tip of each wing under the thicker end to make a neat triangle.

STEP 2. Put the garlic, ginger, soy sauce, lime juice, honey, chilli sauce and oil into a large bowl and mix together.

STEP 3. Put the chicken into the bowl and spoon over the sauce, turning to coat evenly. Cover and marinate for several hours or overnight.

STEP 4. Preheat the grill to hot. Put the wings onto a foil-lined grill pan and cook under the preheated grill, basting frequently with the marinade for 12–15 minutes, or until the juices have no trace of pink. Serve hot with lime wedges.

*Note: Marinate the wings for as long as possible up to 8 hours, to allow the flavours to penetrate the meat.

buffalo wings

Serves 12

Difficulty: Medium

Prep: 20 mins
Cook: 45–50 mins

INGREDIENTS

5 tbsp dark soy sauce

2 tbsp dry sherry

1 tbsp rice vinegar

juice of 1 orange

5-cm/2-inch strip orange
  rind, pith removed

1 tbsp muscovado sugar

1 star anise

1 tsp cornflour, mixed to a
  paste with 3 tbsp water

1 tbsp finely chopped fresh
  ginger

1 tsp chilli sauce

1.5 kg/3 lb 5 oz chicken
  wings

STEP 1. Preheat the oven to 200°C/400°F/Gas Mark 6. Put the soy sauce, sherry, vinegar, orange rind, sugar and star anise into a saucepan, add the orange juice and mix well to combine. Bring to the boil over a medium heat, then stir in the cornflour paste. Continue to boil, stirring constantly, for 1 minute, or until thickened.

STEP 2. Remove from the heat and stir in the ginger and chilli sauce. Remove and discard the tips from the chicken wings and arrange the wings in a single layer in an ovenproof dish or roasting tin. Pour the sauce over the wings, turning and stirring to coat.

STEP 3. Bake in the preheated oven for 35–40 minutes, turning and basting with the sauce occasionally, until the chicken is tender and brown and the juices run clear when a skewer is inserted into the thickest part of the meat. Serve hot or warm.

grilled chicken wings with tahini sauce

Serves 4–6

Difficulty: Medium

Prep: 30 mins, plus 2–24 hours marinating, and 30 mins standing
Cook: 12–15 mins

INGREDIENTS

8 chicken wings, halved

warmed pittas, cut into
fingers, to serve

MARINADE

3 tbsp olive oil

2 tsp smoked Spanish
paprika

1 tsp cumin seeds, crushed

½ tsp dried oregano

2 large garlic cloves, crushed

salt and pepper

TAHINI SAUCE

1 large garlic clove, crushed

¼ tsp salt

125 ml/4 fl oz tahini,
well stirred

juice of 1½ lemons

6–8 tbsp water

STEP 1. Put the chicken wings into a shallow dish. Combine the marinade ingredients and rub into the chicken. Cover and leave to marinate in the refrigerator for 2–24 hours. Remove from the refrigerator and leave to stand 30 minutes before cooking so that they come to room temperature.

STEP 2. To make the sauce, crush the garlic and salt to a paste, using a mortar and pestle. Transfer to a blender with the tahini and lemon juice. Process until smooth, adding enough water to make a creamy sauce. Pour into a serving bowl and set aside.

STEP 3. Preheat the grill. Place the wings on a rack in a foil-lined grill pan and brush with the oily marinade remaining in the dish. Position the pan about 15 cm/ 6 inches from the heat source and grill for 12–15 minutes, turning once, until golden and tender and the juices run clear when a skewer is inserted into the thickest part of the meat. Tip the wings into a serving bowl and pour over the pan juices.

STEP 4. Serve the grilled chicken wings with the tahini sauce and fingers of pitta.

oven-fried chicken wings

Serves 4

Difficulty: Medium
Prep: 20 mins
Cook: 20 mins

INGREDIENTS

12 chicken wings

1 egg

50 ml/2 fl oz milk

4 heaped tbsp plain flour

1 tsp paprika

225 g/8 oz breadcrumbs

55 g/2 oz butter

salt and pepper

STEP 1. Preheat the oven to 220°C/425°F/Gas Mark 7. Separate the chicken wings into three pieces each, discarding the bony tips. Beat the egg with the milk in a shallow dish. Combine the flour, paprika and salt and pepper to taste in a separate shallow dish. Spread the breadcrumbs on a plate.

STEP 2. Dip the chicken pieces into the egg mixture to coat well, then drain and roll in the seasoned flour. Shake off any excess, then roll them in the breadcrumbs, gently pressing the crumbs onto the surface and shaking off any excess.

STEP 3. Put the butter into a shallow roasting tin large enough to hold all the chicken pieces in a single layer and melt in the preheated oven. Arrange the chicken skin side down in the tin and bake in the oven for 10 minutes. Turn and bake for a further 10 minutes, or until the chicken is tender and the juices run clear when a skewer is inserted into the thickest part of the meat.

STEP 4. Remove the chicken from the tin and arrange on a large platter. Serve hot or at room temperature.

asian-style fried chicken

Serves 6–8

Difficulty: Medium

Prep: 20 mins, plus 20 mins marinating
Cook: 26–38 mins

INGREDIENTS

6 skinless, boneless chicken thighs, about 100 g/3½ oz each

4 tbsp shoyu (Japanese soy sauce)

4 tbsp mirin

2 tsp finely grated fresh ginger

2 garlic cloves, crushed

oil, for deep-frying

70 g/2½ oz potato flour or cornflour

pinch of salt

lemon wedges, to serve

STEP 1. Cut the chicken into large cubes and put into a large bowl. Add the shoyu, mirin, ginger and garlic and turn the chicken to coat well. Cover with clingfilm and leave to marinate in a cool place for 20 minutes.

STEP 2. Heat a large wok over a high heat. Pour in the oil and heat to 180°C/350°F, or until a cube of bread browns in 30 seconds.

STEP 3. Meanwhile, mix the potato flour with the salt in a bowl. Lift the chicken out of the marinade and shake off any excess. Drop it into the flour and coat well, then shake off any excess.

STEP 4. Add the chicken to the oil in batches and cook for 6 minutes, or until crisp and brown all over. Remove and drain on kitchen paper, then keep hot while you cook the remaining chicken.

STEP 5. Serve with lemon wedges.

chicken toasts

Serves 4

Difficulty: Easy

Prep: 15 mins
Cook: 10 mins

INGREDIENTS

12 slices French bread or
  rustic bread

4 tbsp olive oil

2 garlic cloves, chopped

2 tbsp finely chopped
  fresh oregano

100 g/3½ oz cold roast
  chicken, cut into small,
  thin slices

4 tomatoes, sliced

12 thin slices goat's cheese

12 black olives, stoned
  and chopped

salt and pepper

fresh green salad leaves,
  to serve

STEP 1. Preheat the oven to 180°C/350°F/Gas Mark 4 and preheat the grill to medium. Place the bread under the preheated grill and lightly toast on both sides. Meanwhile, pour the oil into a bowl and add the garlic and oregano. Season with salt and pepper and mix well. Remove the toasted bread slices from the grill and brush them on one side with the oil mixture.

STEP 2. Place the bread slices oiled side up on a baking sheet. Put some sliced chicken on top of each one, followed by a slice of tomato. Divide the cheese slices between them, then top with the chopped olives. Drizzle over the remaining oil mixture and transfer to the preheated oven. Bake for about 5 minutes, or until the cheese is golden and starting to melt. Remove from the oven and serve with fresh green salad leaves.

*Note: Chicken combines very well with toasted bread and the melted cheese makes these toasts irresistible. You could ring the changes by replacing the goat's cheese and black olives with Cheddar cheese and green olives.

sherried chicken & bacon toasts

Serves 2

Difficulty: Medium

Prep: 25 mins
Cook: 30 mins

INGREDIENTS

2 tbsp olive oil

2 rindless bacon rashers, cut into strips

1 small onion, chopped

2 garlic cloves, chopped

1 bay leaf

2 fresh thyme sprigs

2 small skinless, boneless chicken breasts, cut into small chunks

1 tbsp wholegrain mustard

6 tbsp dry sherry

2 x 2-cm/¾-inch thick slices traditional white bread

25 g/1 oz butter, softened

small handful chopped fresh parsley leaves

2 tbsp natural yogurt (optional)

salt and pepper

STEP 1. Heat the oil in a frying pan and add the bacon, onion, garlic, bay leaf and thyme. Cook, stirring frequently, for 5 minutes until the bacon and onion are cooked. Add the chicken and cook for a further 5 minutes, stirring so that it cooks evenly.

STEP 2. Add the mustard and sherry and bring to the boil, stirring in all the sediment from the base of the pan. Add salt and pepper to taste. Simmer for 3–4 minutes until reduced to a glaze on the ingredients. Discard the bay leaf and herb sprigs.

STEP 3. Meanwhile, preheat the grill to medium-high. Place the bread on a rack in the grill pan and toast for about 2 minutes on each side until golden and crisp.

STEP 4. Butter the toast and place on two warmed plates. Stir the parsley into the chicken mixture and pile it on the toasts. Drizzle over some yogurt, if using, and serve.

creamy chicken

Serves 6

Difficulty: Easy

Prep: 20 mins, plus cooling
Cook: 25 mins

INGREDIENTS

4 tbsp olive oil

900 g/2 lb skinless, boneless
  chicken, diced

125 g/4½ oz rindless smoked
  bacon, diced

12 shallots

2 garlic cloves, crushed

1 tbsp mild curry powder

300 ml/10 fl oz mayonnaise

1 tbsp clear honey

1 tbsp chopped fresh parsley

pepper

85 g/3 oz seedless white
  grapes, quartered,
  to garnish

cold saffron rice, to serve

STEP 1. Heat the oil in a large, heavy-based frying pan. Add the chicken, bacon, shallots, garlic and curry powder. Cook over a low heat, stirring, for about 15 minutes.

STEP 2. Spoon the mixture into a mixing bowl. Leave to cool completely, then season to taste with pepper.

STEP 3. Blend the mayonnaise with the honey, then add the parsley, pour over the chicken mixture and toss well to combine.

STEP 4. Place in a serving dish, garnish with the grapes and serve with cold saffron rice.

*Note: This is a delicious hot weather lunch dish that gets a distinctly Spanish flavour from the saffron rice. It can be made ahead and kept in the fridge for an hour or two before serving, but allow it to come to room temperature for 30 minutes.

chinese lemon chicken

Serves 4

Difficulty: Easy

Prep: 15 mins, plus 15 mins marinating
Cook: 10–12 mins

INGREDIENTS

300 g/10½ oz skinless,
  boneless chicken breast

chopped spring onions,
  to garnish

MARINADE

150 ml/5 fl oz freshly
  squeezed lemon juice

1 tbsp light soy sauce

1 tbsp cornflour

STEP 1. Cut the chicken into bite-sized cubes and place in a shallow dish.

STEP 2. Put the lemon juice and soy sauce into a bowl and mix to combine. Put the cornflour into a separate bowl, stir in the lemon and soy mixture and mix to a paste. Spread over the chicken and leave to marinate for 15 minutes.

STEP 3. Heat a non-stick frying pan and add the chicken and marinade. Cook, stirring, for 10–12 minutes, or until the chicken is thoroughly cooked. Transfer to four warmed serving plates, pour over the sauce and serve, garnished with chopped spring onions.

*Note: You may find it hard to believe that the tasty lemon chicken from your local Chinese takeaway is so quick and easy to prepare and so low in fat. Serve with freshly cooked noodles or jasmine rice to make a more substantial meal.

sautéed chicken with crispy garlic slices

Serves 8

Difficulty: Easy

Prep: 20–30 mins
Cook: 35–40 mins

INGREDIENTS

8 skin-on chicken thighs, boned

hot or sweet smoked Spanish paprika, to taste

4 tbsp Spanish olive oil

10 garlic cloves, sliced

125 ml/4 fl oz dry white wine

1 bay leaf

salt

chopped fresh parsley, to garnish

crusty bread, to serve (optional)

STEP 1. Cut the chicken into bite-sized pieces and season with paprika.

STEP 2. Heat the oil in a large frying pan or flameproof casserole, add the garlic and cook over a medium heat, stirring frequently, for 1 minute until golden brown. Remove with a slotted spoon, drain on kitchen paper and set aside until needed.

STEP 3. Add the chicken to the pan and cook, turning occasionally, for 10 minutes, or until tender and golden brown on all sides. Add the wine and bay leaf and bring to the boil. Reduce the heat and simmer, stirring occasionally, for 10 minutes until the chicken is cooked through. Remove and discard the bay leaf. Season to taste with salt.

STEP 4. Transfer the chicken to a warmed serving dish and sprinkle over the garlic slices. Garnish with chopped parsley and serve with chunks of crusty bread to mop up the juices, if using.

chicken in lemon & garlic

Serves 4

Difficulty: Medium

Prep: 30 mins
Cook: 25–30 mins

INGREDIENTS

4 large skinless, boneless
  chicken breasts

5 tbsp extra virgin olive oil

1 onion, finely chopped

6 garlic cloves, finely
  chopped

grated rind of 1 lemon

juice of 2 lemons

4 tbsp chopped fresh
  flat-leaf parsley

salt and pepper

TO SERVE

finely pared lemon rind

lemon wedges

crusty bread, to serve

STEP 1. Using a sharp knife, slice the chicken breasts widthways into very thin slices. Heat the oil in a large, heavy-based frying pan over a medium heat, add the onion and fry for 5 minutes, or until soft but not brown. Add the garlic and fry for a further 30 seconds.

STEP 2. Add the chicken to the pan and fry gently for 5–10 minutes, stirring occasionally, until all the ingredients are lightly browned and the chicken is tender.

STEP 3. Add the grated lemon rind and lemon juice and leave to bubble, stirring in all the sediment from the base of the pan. Remove the pan from the heat, stir in the parsley and season to taste with salt and pepper.

STEP 4. Transfer the contents of the pan to a warmed serving dish. Sprinkle with pared lemon rind and serve, piping hot, with lemon wedges for squeezing over and crusty bread for mopping up the lemon and garlic juices.

chicken rolls with olives

Serves 4

Difficulty: Medium

Prep: 20 mins
Cook: 45–50 mins

INGREDIENTS

115 g/4 oz black Spanish olives in oil, drained and 2 tbsp oil reserved

140 g/5 oz butter, softened

4 tbsp chopped fresh parsley

4 skinless, boneless chicken breasts

STEP 1. Preheat the oven to 200°C/400°F/Gas Mark 6. Stone and finely chop the olives. Mix the olives, butter and parsley together in a bowl.

STEP 2. Place the chicken breasts between two sheets of clingfilm and gently beat with a meat mallet or the side of a rolling pin.

STEP 3. Spread the olive and herb butter over one side of each flattened chicken breast and roll up. Secure with a wooden cocktail stick or tie with clean string if necessary.

STEP 4. Place the chicken rolls in an ovenproof dish. Drizzle over the oil from the olive jar and bake in the preheated oven for 45–55 minutes, or until tender and the juices run clear when the chicken is pierced with the point of a sharp knife.

STEP 5. Transfer the chicken rolls to a chopping board and discard the cocktail sticks. Cut into slices, then transfer to warmed serving plates and serve.

chicken & corn soup

Serves 6

Difficulty: Easy

Prep: 30 mins, plus soaking
Cook: 1 hour 15 mins

INGREDIENTS

1 roasted chicken, about
  1.3 kg/3 lb

½ tsp saffron threads

3 tbsp corn oil

2 onions, thinly sliced

3 celery sticks, sliced

1.7 litres/3 pints basic
  vegetable stock

8 black peppercorns

1 mace blade

115 g/4 oz egg noodles

400 g/14 oz frozen sweetcorn

pinch of dried sage

2 tbsp chopped fresh parsley

salt and pepper

STEP 1. Remove the skin from the chicken, cut the meat off the bones and cut into small pieces. Put the saffron into a bowl, add enough hot water to cover and leave to soak.

STEP 2. Heat the oil in a saucepan. Add the onions and celery and cook over a low heat, stirring occasionally, for 5 minutes until soft. Increase the heat to medium, pour in the stock, add the peppercorns and mace and bring to the boil. Reduce the heat and simmer for 25 minutes.

STEP 3. Increase the heat to medium, add the chicken, noodles, sweetcorn, sage, parsley and saffron with its soaking water, season to taste with salt and pepper and bring back to the boil. Reduce the heat and simmer for a further 20 minutes.

STEP 4. Remove the pan from the heat, remove the mace blade and adjust the seasoning, if necessary. Ladle into warmed bowls and serve immediately.

chicken & leek soup

Serves 6–8

Difficulty: Medium

Prep: 35 mins
Cook: 1 hour 20 mins–1 hour 50 mins

INGREDIENTS

2 tbsp olive oil

2 onions, roughly chopped

2 carrots, roughly chopped

5 leeks, 2 roughly chopped,
  3 thinly sliced

1 chicken, about 1.3 kg/3 lb

2 bay leaves

6 prunes, sliced

salt and pepper

sprigs of fresh parsley,
  to garnish

STEP 1. Heat the oil in a large saucepan over a medium heat, then add the onions, carrots and the 2 roughly chopped leeks. Sauté for 3–4 minutes until just golden brown. Wipe the chicken inside and out and remove any excess skin and fat.

STEP 2. Add the chicken to the pan with the bay leaves. Pour in enough cold water to just cover and season well with salt and pepper. Bring to the boil, reduce the heat, then cover and simmer for 1–1½ hours. From time to time skim off any foam that rises to the surface.

STEP 3. Remove the chicken from the pan, remove and discard the skin, then take off all the meat. Cut the meat into neat pieces.

STEP 4. Strain the stock through a colander, discard the vegetables and bay leaves and return the stock to the rinsed-out pan. You should have 1.2–1.4 litres/2–2½ pints of stock. Blot the fat off the surface with kitchen paper.

STEP 5. Heat the stock to simmering point, add the sliced leeks and prunes and heat for about 1 minute.

STEP 6. Return the chicken to the pan and heat through. Serve immediately in warmed bowls, garnished with parsley sprigs.

cream of chicken soup

Serves 4

Difficulty: Easy

Prep: 15 mins, plus 10 mins cooling
Cook: 45 mins

INGREDIENTS

3 tbsp butter

4 shallots, chopped

1 leek, sliced

450 g/1 lb skinless, boneless
  chicken breasts, chopped

600 ml/1 pint chicken stock

1 tbsp chopped fresh parsley

1 tbsp chopped fresh thyme,
  plus extra sprigs to garnish

175 ml/6 fl oz double cream

salt and pepper

STEP 1. Melt the butter in a large saucepan over a medium heat. Add the shallots and cook, stirring, for 3 minutes until slightly softened. Add the leek and cook for a further 5 minutes, stirring. Add the chicken, stock, parsley and thyme and season to taste with salt and pepper. Bring to the boil, then reduce the heat and simmer for 25 minutes until the chicken is tender and cooked through. Remove from the heat and leave to cool for 10 minutes.

STEP 2. Transfer the soup to a food processor or blender and process until smooth (you may need to do this in batches). Return the soup to the rinsed-out pan and heat over a low heat for 5 minutes.

STEP 3. Stir in the cream and cook for a further 2 minutes, then remove from the heat and ladle into warmed bowls. Garnish with thyme sprigs and serve immediately.

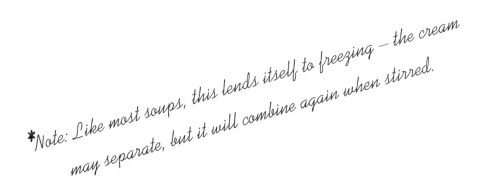

*Note: Like most soups, this lends itself to freezing — the cream may separate, but it will combine again when stirred.

chicken noodle soup

Serves 6–8

Difficulty: Medium

Prep: 30 mins, plus cooling and chilling (optional)
Cook: 50 mins

INGREDIENTS

2 skinless chicken breasts

2 litres/3½ pints water

1 onion, unpeeled, halved

1 large garlic clove, halved

1-cm/½-inch piece fresh
  ginger, peeled and sliced

4 black peppercorns, lightly
  crushed

4 cloves

2 star anise

1 carrot, peeled

1 celery stick, chopped

100 g/3½ oz baby corn,
  halved lengthways

2 spring onions, finely
  shredded

115 g/4 oz dried rice
  vermicelli noodles

salt and pepper

STEP 1. Put the chicken breasts and water into a saucepan over a high heat and bring to the boil. Reduce the heat to low and simmer, skimming the surface until no more foam rises. Add the onion, garlic, ginger, peppercorns, cloves, star anise and a pinch of salt, and continue to simmer for 20 minutes, or until the chicken is tender and cooked through.

STEP 2. Strain the chicken, reserving about 1.2 litres/2 pints of stock, but discarding any solids. (At this point you can leave the stock to cool and chill overnight, so any fat solidifies and can be lifted off and discarded.) Meanwhile, grate the carrot along its length on the coarse side of a grater so you get long, thin strips. Return the stock to the rinsed-out pan with the carrot, celery, baby corn and spring onions and bring to the boil. Boil until the baby corn is almost tender, then add the noodles and continue to boil for a further 2 minutes.

STEP 3. Meanwhile, chop the chicken, add to the pan and continue cooking for a further minute until the chicken is hot and the noodles are soft. Season to taste with salt and pepper, ladle into warmed bowls and serve immediately.

chicken & potato soup with bacon

Serves 4

Difficulty: Easy

Prep: 20 mins
Cook: 45 mins

INGREDIENTS

1 tbsp butter

2 garlic cloves, chopped

1 onion, sliced

250 g/9 oz smoked lean back bacon, chopped

2 large leeks, sliced

2 tbsp plain flour

1 litre/1¾ pints chicken stock

800 g/1 lb 12 oz potatoes, chopped

200 g/7 oz skinless, boneless chicken breast, chopped

50 g/1¾ oz canned sweetcorn

4 tbsp double cream

salt and pepper

grilled bacon, to garnish

STEP 1. Melt the butter in a large saucepan over a medium heat. Add the garlic and onion and cook, stirring, for 3 minutes until slightly softened. Add the bacon and leeks and cook for a further 3 minutes, stirring.

STEP 2. Put the flour into a bowl with enough stock to make a smooth paste, then stir the paste into the pan. Cook, stirring, for 2 minutes. Pour in the remaining stock, then add the potatoes and chicken. Season to taste with salt and pepper. Bring to the boil, then reduce the heat and simmer for 25 minutes until the chicken and potatoes are tender and cooked through.

STEP 3. Stir in the sweetcorn and the cream and cook for a further 2 minutes, then remove from the heat and ladle into warmed serving bowls. Garnish with grilled bacon and serve immediately.

*Note: This hearty soup is a delicious combination of succulent chicken, filling potatoes and smoked bacon. Use single cream if you would prefer it to be slightly less rich.

chicken, prawn & ham soup

Serves 6

Difficulty: Easy

Prep: 20 mins
Cook: 20–25 mins

INGREDIENTS

175 g/6 oz skinless, boneless
  chicken breast, very thinly
  sliced into strips

175 g/6 oz peeled raw
  prawns, halved if large

1 tsp cornflour

2 tsp water

1 small egg white, lightly
  beaten

pinch of salt

1 litre/1¾ pints basic
  vegetable stock

175 g/6 oz honey-roast ham,
  very thinly sliced into strips

salt and pepper

chopped spring onions or
  snipped fresh chives,
  to garnish

STEP 1. Mix the chicken and prawns together in a bowl. Put the cornflour and water into a separate bowl, mix to a paste and add to the chicken and prawns with the egg white and salt, stirring well to coat.

STEP 2. Put the stock into a large saucepan and bring to the boil over a medium heat. Add the chicken mixture and the ham and bring back to the boil. Reduce the heat and simmer for 1 minute. Taste and adjust the seasoning and remove from the heat. Ladle into warmed bowls, garnish with spring onions and serve immediately.

wonton soup

Serves 6

Difficulty: Medium

Prep: 30 mins, plus 20 mins marinating
Cook: 15 mins

INGREDIENTS

175 g/6 oz fresh chicken
  mince

55 g/2 oz raw peeled prawns,
  minced

1 spring onion, finely
  chopped

1 tsp finely chopped fresh
  ginger

1 tsp sugar

1 tbsp Chinese rice wine or
  dry sherry

2 tbsp light soy sauce

24 ready-made wonton
  wrappers

850 ml/1½ pints vegetable
  stock

snipped fresh chives,
  to garnish

STEP 1. Put the chicken, prawns, spring onion, ginger, sugar, rice wine and half the soy sauce into a bowl and mix together until thoroughly combined. Cover and leave to marinate for 20 minutes.

STEP 2. Put 1 teaspoon of the mixture in the centre of each wonton wrapper. Dampen the edges, fold the wrappers corner to corner into a triangle and press to seal, then seal the bottom corners together.

STEP 3. Put the stock into a large saucepan and bring to the boil. Add the wontons and cook for 5 minutes. Stir in the remaining soy sauce and remove from the heat. Ladle the soup and wontons into warmed bowls, sprinkle with snipped chives and serve immediately.

*Note: This is a classic Chinese clear soup — the wontons add delicious flavour and substance. You could replace the chicken mince with fresh pork or duck mince.

smoked chicken & cranberry salad

Serves 4

Difficulty: Medium

Prep: 20 mins, plus chilling and 30 mins soaking
Cook: 12 mins

INGREDIENTS

1 smoked chicken, weighing
   1.3 kg/3 lb

115 g/4 oz dried cranberries

2 tbsp apple juice or water

200 g/7 oz sugar snap peas

2 ripe avocados

juice of ½ lemon

4 lettuce hearts

1 bunch of watercress,
   trimmed

55 g/2 oz rocket

55 g/2 oz chopped walnuts,
   to garnish (optional)

DRESSING

2 tbsp olive oil

1 tbsp walnut oil

2 tbsp lemon juice

1 tbsp chopped fresh mixed
   herbs, such as parsley and
   lemon thyme

salt and pepper

STEP 1. Carve the chicken carefully, slicing the white meat. Divide the legs into thighs and drumsticks and trim the wings. Cover with clingfilm and chill in the refrigerator.

STEP 2. Put the cranberries into a bowl. Stir in the apple juice, cover with clingfilm and leave to soak for 30 minutes.

STEP 3. Meanwhile, blanch the sugar snap peas, refresh under cold running water and drain.

STEP 4. Peel, stone and slice the avocados, then toss in the lemon juice to prevent discoloration.

STEP 5. Separate the lettuce hearts and arrange on a large serving platter with the avocados, sugar snap peas, watercress, rocket and chicken.

STEP 6. To make the dressing, put the olive oil, walnut oil, herbs and salt and pepper to taste into a screw-top jar and shake well to combine.

STEP 7. Drain the cranberries and mix them with the dressing, then pour over the salad.

STEP 8. Serve immediately, scattered with walnuts, if using.

waldorf salad

Serves 4

Difficulty: Easy

Prep: 20 mins, plus 40 mins standing
Cook: None

INGREDIENTS

500 g/1 lb 2 oz red apples, diced

3 tbsp lemon juice

150 ml/5 fl oz mayonnaise

1 head celery

4 shallots, sliced

1 garlic clove, crushed

85 g/3 oz chopped walnuts, plus extra to garnish

500 g/1 lb 2 oz lean cooked chicken, cubed

1 cos lettuce

pepper

STEP 1. Place the apples in a bowl with the lemon juice and 1 tablespoon of the mayonnaise. Leave to stand for 40 minutes, or until needed.

STEP 2. Very thinly slice the celery. Add the celery, shallots, garlic and walnuts to the apples and mix to combine, then add the remaining mayonnaise and mix well together.

STEP 3. Add the chicken, season to taste with pepper and mix to combine.

STEP 4. Line a serving dish with the lettuce. Pile the chicken salad into the dish, garnish with chopped walnuts and serve.

*Note: The original Waldorf salad, created in the late 19th century in the New York hotel of that name, contained no chicken. You could add grapes or dried fruit, substitute the mayonnaise with yogurt, or replace the celery with cauliflower to make an Emerald Waldorf Salad.

cajun chicken salad

Serves 4

Difficulty: Medium

Prep: 30 mins, plus 30 mins chilling
Cook: 15–20 mins

INGREDIENTS

4 skinless, boneless chicken breasts, about 140 g/5 oz each

4 tsp Cajun seasoning

2 tsp sunflower oil

1 ripe mango, peeled, stoned and thickly sliced

200 g/7 oz mixed salad leaves

1 red onion, halved and thinly sliced

175 g/6 oz cooked beetroot, diced

85 g/3 oz radishes, sliced

55 g/2 oz walnut halves

4 tbsp walnut oil

1–2 tsp Dijon mustard

1 tbsp lemon juice

2 tbsp sesame seeds

salt and pepper

STEP 1. Make three diagonal slashes across each chicken breast. Put the chicken into a shallow dish and sprinkle all over with the Cajun seasoning. Cover and chill in the refrigerator for at least 30 minutes.

STEP 2. When ready to cook, brush a griddle pan with the sunflower oil. Heat over a high heat until very hot and a few drops of water sprinkled into the pan sizzle immediately. Add the chicken and cook for 7–8 minutes on each side, or until tender and the juices run clear when a skewer is inserted into the thickest part of the meat. Remove from the pan and set aside until needed.

STEP 3. Add the mango slices to the pan and cook for 2 minutes on each side. Remove from the pan and set aside.

STEP 4. Meanwhile, arrange the salad leaves in a serving bowl and scatter over the onion, beetroot, radishes and walnut halves.

STEP 5. Put the walnut oil, mustard, lemon juice and salt and pepper to taste into a screw-top jar and shake until well blended. Pour over the salad and sprinkle with the sesame seeds.

STEP 6. Cut the chicken into thick slices. Arrange on the salad with the reserved mango slices and serve.

chicken & pancetta caesar salad

Serves 2

Difficulty: Easy

Prep: 20 mins
Cook: 10-15 mins

INGREDIENTS

12 thin smoked pancetta slices

225 g/8 oz skinless, boneless chicken breasts, cubed

1 garlic clove, crushed

3 tbsp olive oil

1 small rustic or ciabatta roll, cut into cubes

1 small cos lettuce, chopped into large pieces

fresh Parmesan cheese shavings, to serve

DRESSING

3 tbsp mayonnaise

2 tbsp soured cream

1 tbsp milk

1 garlic clove, crushed

½ tsp Dijon mustard

2 tbsp finely grated Parmesan cheese

2 anchovy fillets in oil, drained and finely chopped

pepper, to taste

STEP 1. To make the dressing, put all the ingredients into a food processor or blender and process until smooth.

STEP 2. Heat a large non-stick frying pan and add the pancetta. Dry-fry over a high heat for about 2 minutes until crisp and frizzled. Remove with a slotted spoon and drain on kitchen paper. Add the chicken to the pan and fry over a medium-high heat for 5–6 minutes until golden and cooked through. Transfer to the kitchen paper to drain.

STEP 3. Add the garlic and oil to the pan and stir in the bread cubes. Fry over a high heat, turning frequently, for 2–3 minutes until crisp and golden.

STEP 4. Put the lettuce and dressing into a serving bowl and toss together. Add the pancetta and chicken and gently toss. Scatter over the garlic croûtons and Parmesan cheese shavings and serve immediately.

honey & chicken pasta salad

Serves 4

Difficulty: Medium

Prep: 20 mins
Cook: 35–40 mins

INGREDIENTS

250 g/9 oz dried fusilli pasta

2 tbsp olive oil

1 onion, thinly sliced

1 garlic clove, crushed

400 g/14 oz skinless,
    boneless chicken breast,
    thinly sliced

2 tbsp wholegrain mustard

2 tbsp clear honey

175 g/6 oz cherry tomatoes,
    halved

handful of mizuna or rocket
    leaves

fresh thyme leaves,
    to garnish

DRESSING

3 tbsp olive oil

1 tbsp sherry vinegar

2 tsp clear honey

1 tbsp fresh thyme leaves

salt and pepper, to taste

STEP 1. To make the dressing, put all the ingredients into a small bowl and whisk together.

STEP 2. Bring a large saucepan of lightly salted water to the boil, add the pasta, bring back to the boil and cook for 10–12 minutes until just tender but still firm to the bite.

STEP 3. Meanwhile, heat the oil in a large frying pan. Add the onion and garlic and fry for 5 minutes. Add the chicken and cook, stirring frequently, for 3–4 minutes until just cooked through. Stir the mustard and honey into the pan and cook for a further 2–3 minutes until the chicken and onion are golden brown and sticky.

STEP 4. Drain the pasta and transfer to a serving bowl. Pour over the dressing and toss well. Stir in the chicken and onion and leave to cool.

STEP 5. Gently stir the tomatoes and mizuna into the pasta. Serve garnished with the thyme leaves.

layered chicken salad

Serves 4

Difficulty: Medium

Prep: 30 mins, plus cooling
Cook: 25 mins

INGREDIENTS

1 red pepper, halved and
 deseeded

1 green pepper, halved and
 deseeded

2 small courgettes, sliced

750 g/1 lb 10 oz cooked new
 potatoes

1 small onion, thinly sliced

3 tomatoes, sliced

350 g/12 oz cooked chicken,
 sliced

snipped fresh chives,
 to garnish

DRESSING

150 ml/5 fl oz natural yogurt

3 tbsp mayonnaise

1 tbsp snipped fresh chives

salt and pepper

STEP 1. Preheat the grill to high. Place the red peppers skin side up in a grill pan and grill until the skins blacken and begin to char. Remove with tongs, place in a bowl and cover with clingfilm. Set aside until cool enough to handle, then peel off the skins and slice the flesh.

STEP 2. Bring a small saucepan of lightly salted water to the boil, add the courgettes, bring back to the boil and simmer for 3 minutes. Drain, rinse under cold running water to prevent any further cooking and drain again. Set aside until needed.

STEP 3. To make the dressing, put the yogurt, mayonnaise and chives into a small bowl and whisk until well blended. Season to taste with salt and pepper.

STEP 4. Slice the potatoes, add them to the dressing and gently mix to coat evenly. Divide the potatoes between four serving plates.

STEP 5. Top each plate with one quarter of the pepper slices and courgettes. Layer one quarter of the onion and tomato slices, then the sliced chicken, on top of each serving. Garnish with chives and serve immediately.

chicken & cheese salad

Serves 4

Difficulty: Easy

Prep: 20 mins

Cook: None

INGREDIENTS

150 g/5½ oz rocket leaves

2 celery sticks, trimmed and sliced

½ cucumber, sliced

2 spring onions, trimmed and sliced

2 tbsp chopped fresh flat-leaf parsley

25 g/1 oz walnut pieces

350 g/12 oz boneless roast chicken, sliced

125 g/4½ oz Stilton cheese, cubed

handful of seedless red grapes, halved (optional)

salt and pepper

DRESSING

2 tbsp olive oil

1 tbsp sherry vinegar

1 tsp Dijon mustard

1 tbsp chopped mixed herbs

STEP 1. Wash the rocket leaves, pat dry with kitchen paper and put them into a large salad bowl. Add the celery, cucumber, spring onions, parsley and walnuts and mix well together. Transfer to a large serving platter. Arrange the chicken slices over the salad, then scatter over the cheese. Add the grapes, if using, and season well with salt and pepper.

STEP 2. To make the dressing, put all the ingredients into a small screw-top jar and shake until well blended. Drizzle the dressing over the salad and serve.

*Note: This salad uses Stilton cheese, but you could replace it with a creamy Gorgonzola if you prefer a milder flavour.

roast chicken with pesto cream salad

Serves 6–8

Difficulty: Easy

Prep: 20 mins, plus chilling
Cook: None

INGREDIENTS

600 g/1 lb 5 oz skinless,
  boneless cooked chicken,
  cut into bite-sized pieces

3 celery sticks, chopped

2 large peeled red peppers
  from a jar, well drained and
  sliced

salt and pepper

iceberg lettuce leaves,
  to serve

PESTO CREAM

150 ml/5 fl oz crème fraîche
  or soured cream

4 tbsp bottled green pesto

STEP 1. To make the pesto cream, put the crème fraîche into a large bowl, then beat in the pesto.

STEP 2. Add the chicken, celery and red peppers to the bowl and gently toss together. Add salt and pepper to taste and toss again. Cover and chill until required.

STEP 3. Remove the salad from the refrigerator 10 minutes before serving to allow it to come to room temperature. Give the salad ingredients a good stir, then divide between individual plates lined with lettuce leaves.

*Note: Add more pesto to the dressing if you'd like a stronger flavour of basil — or replace the green pesto with red pesto.

lunches & light bites

mediterranean pan bagnat

Serves 6–8

Difficulty: Easy

Prep: 15 mins
Cook: None

INGREDIENTS

1 garlic clove, halved

1 large baguette,
  cut lengthways

4 tbsp olive oil

140 g/5 oz cold roast
  chicken, thinly sliced

2 large tomatoes, sliced

20 g/¾ oz canned anchovy
  fillets, drained

8 large black olives, stoned
  and chopped

pepper

STEP 1. Rub the garlic over the cut sides of the bread and sprinkle with the oil.

STEP 2. Arrange the chicken on top of the bread. Arrange the tomatoes and anchovies on top of the chicken.

STEP 3. Scatter with the black olives and season with plenty of pepper. Sandwich the loaf back together and wrap tightly in foil until required. Cut into slices to serve.

*Note: This is a favourite packed lunch in southern provincial France. It literally means 'wet bread', and the filled bread is tightly wrapped in foil so that the oil can seep into it. You could vary the ingredients with roasted red peppers, courgettes and aubergines and chopped sun-dried tomatoes.

open chicken sandwiches

Serves 6–8

Difficulty: Easy

Prep: 15 mins

Cook: None

INGREDIENTS

3 hard-boiled eggs, yolks mashed and whites chopped

25 g/1 oz butter, softened

2 tbsp English mustard

1 tsp anchovy extract

250 g/9 oz Cheddar cheese, grated

3 cooked skinless, boneless chicken breasts, diced

6 thick slices rustic bread, buttered

12 tomato slices

12 cucumber slices

pepper

STEP 1. Put the egg yolks and whites into a large bowl with the butter, mustard and anchovy extract. Season to taste with pepper and mix to combine.

STEP 2. Mix in the cheese and chicken and spread the mixture on the bread.

STEP 3. Arrange the tomato and cucumber slices on top of the egg and chicken mixture and serve.

*Note: Anchovy extract is widely used in Italy, where food is never seasoned at the table. It gives a rich depth of flavour and packs a very salty punch, so don't be tempted to add any additional salt to the sandwich.

smoked chicken & ham focaccia

Serves 2–4

Difficulty: Medium

Prep: 20 mins
Cook: 5 mins

INGREDIENTS

1 thick focaccia loaf (about 15–17.5 cm/6–7 inches)

handful of basil leaves

2 small courgettes, coarsely grated

6 wafer-thin slices of smoked chicken

6 wafer-thin slices of cooked ham

225 g/8 oz Taleggio cheese, cut into strips

freshly grated nutmeg (optional)

cherry tomatoes, to serve

STEP 1. Preheat a griddle or grill pan under the grill until hot. Slice the focaccia in half horizontally and cut the top half lengthways into strips.

STEP 2. Cover the bottom half of the focaccia with basil leaves, top with the courgettes in an even layer and then cover with the chicken and ham, alternating the slices and wrinkling them as you place them. Lay the strips of focaccia on top, placing strips of the cheese between them. Sprinkle with a little nutmeg, if using.

STEP 3. Transfer to the hot griddle and cook under the grill, at a good distance from the heat, for 5 minutes until the cheese has melted and the top of the bread is brown. Cut the bread crossways into four pieces and serve immediately with cherry tomatoes.

chicken & mushroom pizza

Serves 2–4

Difficulty: Easy

Prep: 20 mins, plus cooling
Cook: 30 mins

INGREDIENTS

4 tbsp olive oil, plus extra for brushing

2 shallots, thinly sliced

1 yellow pepper, deseeded and cut into thin strips

115 g/4 oz chestnut mushrooms, thinly sliced

350 g/12 oz skinless, boneless chicken breast portions, cut into thin strips

1 x 25-cm/10-inch pizza base

2 tbsp chopped fresh parsley

175 g/6 oz mozzarella cheese, grated

salt and pepper

STEP 1. Preheat the oven to 200°C/400°F/Gas Mark 6. Brush a baking sheet with oil.

STEP 2. Heat 2 tablespoons of the oil in a wok or large frying pan. Add the shallots, yellow pepper, mushrooms and chicken and stir-fry over a medium-high heat for 4–5 minutes. Transfer the mixture to a plate with a slotted spoon and leave to cool.

STEP 3. Brush the pizza base with 1 tablespoon of the olive oil. Stir the parsley into the chicken and mushroom mixture and season with salt and pepper. Spread the mixture evenly over the pizza base almost to the edge. Sprinkle with the mozzarella, drizzle over the remaining olive oil, and bake in the preheated oven for 20 minutes until the edge is crisp and golden. Serve immediately.

*Note: A pizza without any tomato sauce on the base is known as a 'pizza bianca', or white pizza. More oil is needed to keep white pizzas moist during cooking, so be generous!

chicken wraps

Serves 4

Difficulty: Easy

Prep: 20 mins

Cook: None

INGREDIENTS

150 g/5½ oz natural yogurt

1 tbsp wholegrain mustard

280 g/10 oz cooked skinless, boneless chicken breast, diced

140 g/5 oz iceberg lettuce, finely shredded

85 g/3 oz cucumber, thinly sliced

2 celery sticks, sliced

85 g/3 oz black seedless grapes, halved

8 x 20-cm/8-inch soft flour tortillas or 4 x 25-cm/ 10-inch soft flour tortillas

pepper

STEP 1. Put the yogurt and mustard into a bowl, stir to combine and season to taste with pepper. Stir in the chicken and toss until thoroughly coated.

STEP 2. Put the lettuce, cucumber, celery and grapes into a separate bowl and mix well together.

STEP 3. Fold a tortilla in half and in half again to make a cone that is easy to hold. Half-fill the tortilla pocket with the salad mixture and top with some of the chicken mixture. Repeat with the remaining tortillas, salad and chicken. Serve immediately.

*Note: These are very easy to make and children love preparing them. You can use any ingredients you like for the filling, from leftover chicken tikka masala to thinly sliced roast beef. Make sure to include plenty of crunchy lettuce, cucumber and celery.

chicken fajitas

Serves 4

Difficulty: Medium

Prep: 15 mins, plus 2–3 hours chilling
Cook: 10–15 mins

INGREDIENTS

3 tbsp olive oil, plus extra for drizzling

3 tbsp maple syrup or clear honey

1 tbsp red wine vinegar

2 garlic cloves, crushed

2 tsp dried oregano

1–2 tsp dried chilli flakes

4 skinless, boneless chicken breasts

2 red peppers, deseeded and cut into 2.5-cm/1-inch strips

salt and pepper

warmed flour tortillas and shredded lettuce, to serve

STEP 1. Put the oil, maple syrup, vinegar, garlic, oregano, chilli flakes and salt and pepper to taste into a large, shallow dish or bowl and mix together.

STEP 2. Slice the chicken across the grain into 2.5-cm/ 1-inch thick slices, then toss in the marinade until well coated. Cover and chill in the refrigerator for 2–3 hours, turning occasionally.

STEP 3. Heat a griddle pan until hot. Lift the chicken slices from the marinade with a slotted spoon, place on the griddle pan and cook over a medium-high heat for 3–4 minutes on each side, or until cooked through. Transfer the chicken to a warmed plate and keep warm.

STEP 4. Place the peppers skin side down on the pan and cook for 2 minutes on each side. Transfer to the plate with the chicken.

STEP 5. Divide the chicken and peppers between the flour tortillas, top with a little shredded lettuce, wrap and serve immediately.

the ultimate chicken burger

Serves 4

Difficulty: Medium

Prep: 25 mins, plus 30 mins chilling
Cook: 18–20 mins

INGREDIENTS

4 large skinless, boneless
  chicken breasts

1 large egg white

1 tbsp cornflour

1 tbsp plain flour

1 egg, beaten

55 g/2 oz fresh white
  breadcrumbs

2 tbsp sunflower oil

2 beef tomatoes, sliced

TO SERVE

4 burger buns, sliced

shredded lettuce

mayonnaise

STEP 1. Place the chicken breasts between two sheets of non-stick baking paper and flatten slightly with a meat mallet or a rolling pin. Put the egg white and cornflour into a small bowl and beat together, then brush over the chicken. Cover and leave to chill for 30 minutes, then coat in the plain flour.

STEP 2. Put the egg and breadcrumbs into two separate wide, shallow bowls and coat the burgers first in the egg, allowing any excess to drip back into the bowl, and then in the breadcrumbs, shaking off the excess.

STEP 3. Heat the oil in a heavy-based frying pan over a medium heat, add the burgers and cook for 6–8 minutes on each side, or until cooked through. Add the tomato slices for the last 1–2 minutes of the cooking time.

STEP 4. Serve the burgers in the buns with the tomato slices, a little shredded lettuce and some mayonnaise.

bacon-wrapped chicken burgers

Serves 4

Difficulty: Medium

Prep: 20 mins, plus 1 hour chilling
Cook: 15–18 mins

INGREDIENTS

450 g/1 lb fresh chicken
    mince

1 onion, grated

2 garlic cloves, crushed

55 g/2 oz pine nuts, toasted

55 g/2 oz Gruyère cheese,
    grated

2 tbsp snipped fresh chives

2 tbsp wholemeal flour

8 lean back rashers

1–2 tbsp sunflower oil

salt and pepper

TO SERVE

4 crusty rolls, sliced

red onion slices

chopped lettuce

mayonnaise

chopped spring onions

STEP 1. Put the chicken, onion, garlic, pine nuts, cheese and chives into a food processor with salt and pepper to taste. Pulse until combined. Scrape out onto a board and shape into four burgers. Coat in the flour, then cover and chill for 1 hour.

STEP 2. Wrap each burger with 2 bacon rashers, securing in place with a wooden cocktail stick.

STEP 3. Heat a heavy-based frying pan and add the oil. When hot, add the burgers and cook over a medium heat for 5–6 minutes on each side, or until thoroughly cooked.

STEP 4. Serve the burgers in the crusty rolls with red onion slices, chopped lettuce, a spoonful of mayonnaise and chopped spring onions.

*Note: Do make sure that the burgers are properly cooked. Insert a sharp knife into the middle of a burger – if the juices run clear, the burgers are cooked.

chicken nuggets

Serves 4

Difficulty: Medium

Prep. 30 mins
Cook: 25–30 mins

INGREDIENTS

3 skinless, boneless chicken
  breasts

4 tbsp wholemeal flour

1 tbsp wheatgerm

½ tsp ground cumin

½ tsp ground coriander

1 egg, lightly beaten

2 tbsp olive oil

pepper

DIPPING SAUCE

100 g/3½ oz sun-blush
  tomatoes

100 g/3½ oz fresh tomatoes,
  peeled, deseeded and
  chopped

2 tbsp mayonnaise

STEP 1. Preheat the oven to 190°C/375°F/Gas Mark 5. Cut the chicken breasts into 4-cm/1½-inch chunks. Put the flour, wheatgerm, cumin, coriander and pepper to taste into a bowl and mix well together, then divide between two separate plates. Put the beaten egg on a third plate.

STEP 2. Pour the oil into a baking tray and heat in the preheated oven. Roll the chicken pieces in one plate of flour, shake to remove any excess, then roll in the egg and in the second plate of flour, shaking off the excess. When all the nuggets are coated, remove the tray from the oven and toss the nuggets in the hot oil. Roast in the oven for 25–30 minutes until golden and crisp.

STEP 3. Meanwhile, to make the dipping sauce, put the sun-blush tomatoes and fresh tomatoes into a blender or food processor and process until smooth. Add the mayonnaise and process again until well combined.

STEP 4. Remove the nuggets from the oven and drain on kitchen paper. Serve with the dipping sauce.

jerk chicken

Serves 4

Difficulty: Easy

Prep: 30 mins, plus 8 hours marinating
Cook: 30–35 mins

INGREDIENTS

2 fresh red chillies

2 tbsp corn oil, plus extra for
  brushing

2 garlic cloves, finely
  chopped

1 tbsp finely chopped onion

1 tbsp finely chopped spring
  onion

1 tbsp white wine vinegar

1 tbsp lime juice

2 tsp demerara sugar

1 tsp dried thyme

1 tsp ground cinnamon

1 tsp ground mixed spice

¼ tsp freshly grated nutmeg

4 chicken quarters

salt and pepper

fresh coriander sprigs and
  lime wedges, to garnish

STEP 1. Deseed and finely chop the chillies, then put them into a small glass bowl with the oil, garlic, onion, spring onion, vinegar, lime juice, sugar, thyme, cinnamon, mixed spice and nutmeg. Season to taste with salt and pepper and mash thoroughly with a fork.

STEP 2. Using a sharp knife, make a series of diagonal slashes in the chicken pieces and place them in a large, shallow, non-metallic dish. Spoon the marinade over the chicken, rubbing it well into the slashes. Cover and leave to marinate in the refrigerator for up to 8 hours.

STEP 3. Preheat the grill. Remove the chicken from the marinade, discarding the marinade, brush with oil and cook under the preheated grill, turning frequently, for 30–35 minutes. Transfer to plates and serve garnished with coriander sprigs and lime wedges.

mustard & honey drumsticks

Serves 4

Difficulty: Easy

Prep: 15 mins, plus 1 hour marinating
Cook: 25–30 mins

INGREDIENTS

8 chicken drumsticks

fresh parsley sprigs,
  to garnish

GLAZE

125 ml/4 fl oz clear honey

4 tbsp Dijon mustard

4 tbsp wholegrain mustard

4 tbsp white wine vinegar

2 tbsp sunflower oil

salt and pepper, to taste

STEP 1. Using a sharp knife, make 2–3 diagonal slashes in the chicken drumsticks and place them in a large, non-metallic dish.

STEP 2. To make the glaze, put all the ingredients into a jug and mix to combine. Pour the glaze over the drumsticks, turning until well coated. Cover with clingfilm and marinate in the refrigerator for at least 1 hour.

STEP 3. Preheat the grill. Drain the chicken, reserving the marinade. Cook the chicken under the preheated grill, turning frequently and brushing with the reserved marinade, for 25–30 minutes, or until thoroughly cooked. Transfer to serving plates, garnish with parsley sprigs and serve immediately.

*Note: To prevent charring, wrap any protruding chicken bones in foil before placing the drumsticks under the grill.

chicken croquettes

Serves 4

Difficulty: Medium

Prep: 40 mins, plus 1 hour chilling
Cook: 1 hour 10 mins

INGREDIENTS

6 tbsp olive oil

1 onion, finely chopped

1 celery stick, finely chopped

225 g/8 oz cooked chicken,
  finely chopped

3 tomatoes

550 g/1 lb 4 oz boiled
  potatoes, finely chopped

plain flour, for dusting

2 eggs, lightly beaten

115 g/4 oz dry breadcrumbs

1 tbsp chopped fresh parsley

RICH TOMATO SAUCE

1 lean bacon rasher

25 g/1 oz butter

1 shallot, finely chopped

1 garlic clove, finely chopped

1 celery stick, finely chopped

1 carrot, finely chopped

400 g/14 oz canned chopped
  tomatoes

2 tsp cornflour

300 ml/10 fl oz chicken stock

salt and pepper

STEP 1. Heat half the oil in a saucepan. Add the onion and celery and cook over a low heat, stirring occasionally, for 5 minutes until soft. Add the chicken, tomatoes and potatoes and cook, stirring frequently, for 8–10 minutes. Transfer the mixture to a food processor and process until smooth. Scrape into a bowl and leave to cool, then chill for 1 hour.

STEP 2. Meanwhile, make the sauce. Remove the bacon rind and dice the bacon. Melt the butter with the bacon rind in a saucepan. Add the bacon, shallot, garlic, celery and carrot and cook over a low heat, stirring occasionally, for 5 minutes. Stir in the tomatoes and cook, stirring occasionally, for 5 minutes. Stir the cornflour into the stock and pour it into the pan. Season to taste with salt and pepper. Cover and simmer, stirring occasionally, for 20 minutes until thickened. Remove and discard the bacon rind.

STEP 3. Lightly dust your hands with flour and divide the chicken mixture into 8–12 pieces. Roll each into a small croquette. Put the beaten eggs into a shallow bowl and spread out the breadcrumbs in a separate shallow bowl. Dip the croquettes into the egg, then into the breadcrumbs, turning to coat.

STEP 4. Heat the remaining oil in a frying pan. Add the croquettes and cook over a medium heat, turning once, for 10 minutes. Drain on kitchen paper. Pour the sauce over the croquettes, sprinkle with parsley and serve.

chicken & chilli enchiladas

Serves 4

Difficulty: Medium

Prep: 30 mins

Cook: 35 mins

INGREDIENTS

corn oil, for brushing

5 fresh hot green chillies, such as jalapeño, deseeded and chopped

1 Spanish onion, chopped

2 garlic cloves, chopped

2 tbsp chopped fresh coriander

2 tbsp lime juice

125 ml/4 fl oz chicken stock

2 beef tomatoes, peeled, deseeded and chopped

pinch of sugar

350 g/12 oz cooked chicken, shredded

85 g/3 oz queso añejo or Cheddar cheese, grated

2 tsp chopped fresh oregano

8 corn tortillas or flour tortillas

salt

STEP 1. Preheat the oven to 180°C/350°F/Gas Mark 4 and brush a large, ovenproof dish with oil. Put two thirds of the chillies, the onion, garlic, coriander, lime juice, stock, tomatoes and sugar into a food processor and pulse to a purée. Scrape into a saucepan and simmer over a medium heat for 10 minutes until thickened.

STEP 2. Mix the remaining chillies, the chicken, 55 g/2 oz of the cheese and the oregano together. Season to taste with salt and stir in half the sauce.

STEP 3. Heat the tortillas in a dry, heavy-based frying pan or heat in the microwave according to the packet instructions. Divide the chicken mixture between the tortillas, spooning it along the centres, then roll up and place seam side down in the prepared dish.

STEP 4. Pour the remaining sauce over the enchiladas and sprinkle with the remaining cheese. Bake in the preheated oven for 20 minutes and serve hot.

zesty chicken kebabs

Serves 6–8

Difficulty: Medium

Prep: 30 mins, plus 8 hours marinating
Cook: 6–10 mins

INGREDIENTS

4 skinless, boneless chicken
  breasts, about 175 g/6 oz
  each

finely grated rind and juice
  of ½ lemon

finely grated rind and juice
  of ½ orange

2 tbsp clear honey

2 tbsp olive oil

2 tbsp chopped fresh mint

¼ tsp ground coriander

salt and pepper

STEP 1. Using a sharp knife, cut the chicken into 2.5-cm/1-inch cubes, then put into a large glass bowl. Put the lemon rind and juice, the orange rind and juice, honey, oil, mint and coriander into a jug and mix together. Season to taste with salt and pepper. Pour the marinade over the chicken and toss until thoroughly coated. Cover with clingfilm and leave to marinate in the refrigerator for up to 8 hours.

STEP 2. Preheat the barbecue or grill. Drain the chicken, reserving the marinade. Thread the chicken onto eight metal or pre-soaked wooden skewers.

STEP 3. Cook the skewers over medium-hot coals or under the preheated grill, turning and basting frequently with the reserved marinade, for 6–10 minutes, or until cooked through. Transfer to a large serving plate and serve immediately.

cajun chicken

Serves 4

Difficulty: Medium

Prep: 30 mins
Cook: 25–30 mins

INGREDIENTS

4 chicken drumsticks

4 chicken thighs

2 fresh corn cobs, husks and
  silks removed

85 g/3 oz butter, melted

fresh flat-leaf parsley sprigs,
  to garnish

SPICE MIX

2 tsp onion powder

2 tsp paprika

1½ tsp salt

1 tsp garlic powder

1 tsp dried thyme

1 tsp cayenne pepper

1 tsp ground black pepper

½ tsp ground white pepper

¼ tsp ground cumin

STEP 1. Preheat the barbecue or grill to medium-hot. Using a sharp knife, make 2–3 diagonal slashes in the chicken drumsticks and thighs, then put them into a large dish. Cut the corn into thick slices and add to the dish. Put all the ingredients for the spice mix into a small bowl and mix together.

STEP 2. Brush the chicken and corn with the melted butter and sprinkle with the spice mix. Toss to coat well.

STEP 3. Cook the chicken on the preheated barbecue, turning occasionally, for 15 minutes, then add the corn and cook, turning occasionally, for a further 10–15 minutes, or until beginning to blacken slightly at the edges. Transfer to a large serving plate, garnish with parsley and serve immediately.

*Note: The blackening on the corn shows that it is caramelizing — it should not be cooked for any longer or it will dry out.

chicken kiev

Serves 6–8

Difficulty: Medium

Prep: 30 mins, plus 3 hours chilling
Cook: 26–30 mins

INGREDIENTS

115 g/4 oz butter, softened

3–4 garlic cloves, very finely
  chopped

1 tbsp chopped fresh parsley

1 tbsp snipped fresh chives

finely grated rind and juice
  of ½ lemon

8 skinless, boneless chicken
  breasts, about 115 g/4 oz
  each

55 g/2 oz plain flour

2 eggs, lightly beaten

175 g/6 oz dry breadcrumbs

groundnut oil or sunflower
  oil, for deep-frying

salt and pepper

STEP 1. Beat the butter in a bowl with the garlic, herbs and lemon rind and juice. Season to taste with salt and pepper. Divide into eight portions, then shape each portion into a cylinder. Wrap in foil and chill for about 2 hours until firm.

STEP 2. Place the chicken between two sheets of clingfilm and gently pound with a rolling pin to flatten to an even thickness. Place a butter cylinder on each piece and roll up. Secure with wooden cocktail sticks.

STEP 3. Put the flour, eggs and breadcrumbs into separate shallow dishes. Dip the rolls in the flour, then the egg and, finally, the breadcrumbs. Place on a plate, cover and chill for 1 hour.

STEP 4. Heat the oil in a large saucepan or deep-fat fryer to 180°C/350°F, or until a cube of bread browns in 30 seconds. Add the chicken in batches and deep-fry for 8–10 minutes, or until cooked through and golden brown. Drain on kitchen paper. Carefully remove the cocktail sticks and serve immediately.

spicy chicken & tomato kebabs

Serves 4

Difficulty: Easy

Prep: 20 mins
Cook: 8–10 mins

INGREDIENTS

500 g/1 lb 2 oz skinless,
  boneless chicken breasts

3 tbsp tomato purée

2 tbsp clear honey

2 tbsp Worcestershire sauce

1 tbsp chopped fresh
  rosemary

250 g/9 oz cherry tomatoes

STEP 1. Using a sharp knife, cut the chicken into small chunks and put into a large bowl. Put the tomato purée, honey, Worcestershire sauce and rosemary into a separate bowl and mix together, then add to the chicken, stirring to coat evenly.

STEP 2. Preheat the barbecue or grill to medium-hot. Drain the chicken, reserving the marinade. Thread the chicken pieces and cherry tomatoes alternately onto eight metal or pre-soaked wooden skewers.

STEP 3. Cook the kebabs on the preheated barbecue, turning occasionally and basting with the reserved marinade, for 8–10 minutes until the chicken is cooked through. Transfer to a plate and serve immediately.

chicken with tarragon butter

Serves 4

Difficulty: Medium

Prep: 30 mins, plus chilling, 30 mins marinating and 5 mins resting
Cook: 9–11 mins

INGREDIENTS

4 skinless, boneless chicken
 breasts, about 225 g/8 oz
 each

oil, for oiling

TARRAGON BUTTER

100 g/3½ oz unsalted butter,
 at room temperature

5 tbsp chopped fresh
 tarragon

1 shallot, finely chopped

salt and pepper

MARINADE

1½ tbsp lemon juice

2 tbsp water

1 tsp sugar

1 tsp salt

½ tsp pepper

3 tbsp olive oil

STEP 1. Preheat the barbecue to medium-hot. To make the tarragon butter, mash the butter with a fork until soft, then add the tarragon, shallot and salt and pepper to taste, mixing well. Scrape the mixture onto a piece of clingfilm and shape into a log. Wrap tightly and chill in the refrigerator.

STEP 2. Meanwhile, slice the chicken breasts lengthways to make 8 pieces. Place in a shallow dish in a single layer. Mix the marinade ingredients together and pour over the chicken. Cover with clingfilm and leave to marinate in the refrigerator for 30 minutes, turning halfway through.

STEP 3. Drain the chicken, discarding the marinade. Pat dry and lightly brush with oil. Oil the grill rack. Place the chicken on the rack and cover with a disposable foil tray. Cook for 5–6 minutes until the underside is striped with grill marks and is no longer translucent. Turn and cook the other side for 4–5 minutes, or until cooked through.

STEP 4. Place in a warmed dish, cover with foil and leave to rest in a warm place for 5 minutes. Serve with slices of the tarragon butter.

yaki soba

Serves 2

Difficulty: Easy

Prep: 20 mins
Cook: 10 mins

INGREDIENTS

400 g/14 oz ramen noodles

1 onion, finely sliced

200 g/7 oz beansprouts

1 red pepper, deseeded and
sliced

150 g/5½ oz cooked chicken,
sliced

12 cooked peeled prawns

1 tbsp oil, for stir-frying

2 tbsp shoyu

½ tbsp mirin

1 tsp sesame oil

1 tsp sesame seeds

2 spring onions, finely sliced

STEP 1. Cook the noodles according to the packet instructions, drain well and tip into a bowl.

STEP 2. Mix the onion, beansprouts, red pepper, chicken and prawns together in a bowl. Stir through the noodles. Meanwhile, preheat a wok over a high heat, add the oil and heat until very hot.

STEP 3. Add the noodle mixture and stir-fry for 4 minutes, or until golden, then add the shoyu, mirin and sesame oil and toss together.

STEP 4. Divide the noodles between two bowls. Sprinkle with sesame seeds and spring onions and serve.

*Note: This is a very quick and easy recipe when you have some leftover roast chicken in the fridge – however, it's tasty enough to be worth the effort of roasting a chicken portion specially.

chicken fried rice

Serves 4

Difficulty: Easy

Prep: 20 mins
Cook: 20–25 mins

INGREDIENTS

½ tbsp sesame oil

6 shallots, peeled and cut
  into quarters

450 g/1 lb cooked chicken,
  cubed

3 tbsp soy sauce

2 carrots, diced

1 celery stick, diced

1 red pepper, deseeded and
  diced

175 g/6 oz fresh peas

100 g/3½ oz canned
  sweetcorn, drained

275 g/9¾ oz cooked
  long-grain rice

2 large eggs, beaten

STEP 1. Heat the oil in a preheated wok or large frying pan over a medium heat.

STEP 2. Add the shallots and fry until soft, then add the chicken and 2 tablespoons of the soy sauce and stir-fry for 5–6 minutes.

STEP 3. Stir in the carrots, celery, red pepper, peas and sweetcorn and stir-fry for a further 5 minutes.

STEP 4. Add the rice and stir thoroughly. Add the eggs and stir until they are beginning to set, then add the remaining soy sauce.

STEP 5. Transfer to bowls and serve immediately.

sweet & sour chicken

Serves 4–6

Difficulty: Medium

Prep: 25 mins, plus 20 mins marinating
Cook: 25–30 mins

INGREDIENTS

450 g/1 lb lean chicken,
 cubed

5 tbsp vegetable or
 groundnut oil

½ tsp crushed garlic

½ tsp finely chopped fresh
 ginger

1 green pepper, deseeded
 and roughly chopped

1 onion, roughly chopped

1 carrot, finely sliced

1 tsp sesame oil

1 tbsp finely chopped spring
 onion

freshly cooked plain rice,
 to serve

MARINADE

2 tsp light soy sauce

1 tsp Chinese rice wine

pinch of white pepper

½ tsp salt

dash of sesame oil

SAUCE

8 tbsp rice vinegar

4 tbsp sugar

2 tsp light soy sauce

6 tbsp tomato ketchup

STEP 1. Combine all the marinade ingredients in a bowl, add the chicken and marinate for at least 20 minutes.

STEP 2. To make the sauce, heat the vinegar in a small saucepan and add the sugar, soy sauce and tomato ketchup. Stir to dissolve the sugar, then remove from the heat and set aside until needed.

STEP 3. Heat a wok over a high heat, then add 3 tablespoons of the vegetable oil. Add the chicken and stir-fry until it starts to turn golden brown. Remove and set aside. Wipe the wok clean with kitchen paper.

STEP 4. Reheat the wok over a high heat, add the remaining vegetable oil, the garlic and ginger and cook until fragrant. Add the green pepper, onion and carrot and cook for 2 minutes. Add the chicken and cook for a further minute. Add the sauce and the sesame oil, then stir in the spring onion and serve immediately with rice.

chicken chow mein

Serves 4

Difficulty: Easy
Prep: 20 mins
Cook: 15 mins

INGREDIENTS

250 g/9 oz medium egg
  noodles

2 tbsp sunflower oil

275 g/9¾ oz cooked chicken
  breasts, shredded

1 garlic clove, finely chopped

1 red pepper, deseeded and
  thinly sliced

100 g/3½ oz shiitake
  mushrooms, sliced

6 spring onions, sliced

100 g/3½ oz beansprouts

3 tbsp soy sauce

1 tbsp sesame oil

STEP 1. Put the noodles into a large bowl and break them up slightly. Pour over enough boiling water to cover and leave to stand while preparing the remaining ingredients.

STEP 2. Heat the sunflower oil in a large preheated wok. Add the chicken, garlic, red pepper, mushrooms, spring onions and beansprouts to the wok and stir-fry for about 5 minutes.

STEP 3. Drain the noodles thoroughly. Add the noodles to the wok, toss well and stir-fry for a further 5 minutes.

STEP 4. Drizzle the soy sauce and sesame oil over the chow mein and toss until well combined.

STEP 5. Transfer to warmed bowls and serve.

*Note: Canned water chestnuts are often included in chow mein dishes. If you need to bulk up this recipe, add 200 g/7 oz to the wok with the noodles in Step 3.

chicken with pak choi

Serves 4

Difficulty: Easy

Prep: 25 mins
Cook: 25–30 mins

INGREDIENTS

175 g/6 oz broccoli florets

1 tbsp groundnut oil

2.5-cm/1-inch piece fresh
ginger, finely grated

1 fresh red Thai chilli,
deseeded and chopped

2 garlic cloves, crushed

1 red onion, cut into wedges

450 g/1 lb skinless, boneless
chicken breast, cut into thin
strips

175 g/6 oz pak choi,
shredded

115 g/4 oz baby corn, halved

1 tbsp light soy sauce

1 tbsp Thai fish sauce

1 tbsp chopped fresh
coriander

1 tbsp toasted sesame seeds

salt

STEP 1. Bring a saucepan of lightly salted water to the boil, add the broccoli, bring back to the boil and cook for 3 minutes. Drain and set aside.

STEP 2. Heat a wok over a high heat until almost smoking. Add the oil, then add the ginger, chilli and garlic and stir-fry for 1 minute. Add the onion and chicken and stir-fry for a further 3–4 minutes, or until the chicken is sealed on all sides.

STEP 3. Add the pak choi, baby corn and broccoli to the wok and stir-fry for 3–4 minutes, or until tender.

STEP 4. Add the soy sauce and Thai fish sauce to the wok and stir-fry for a further 1–2 minutes, then sprinkle with the coriander and sesame seeds and serve.

quick chicken laksa

Serves 4

Difficulty: Easy

Prep: 20 mins
Cook: 25–30 mins

INGREDIENTS

850 ml/1½ pints canned
   coconut milk

200 ml/7 fl oz chicken stock

2–3 tbsp laksa paste

3 skinless, boneless chicken
   breasts, about 175 g/6 oz
   each, sliced into strips

250 g/9 oz cherry tomatoes,
   halved

250 g/9 oz sugar snap peas,
   halved diagonally

200 g/7 oz dried rice noodles

1 bunch fresh coriander,
   roughly chopped

STEP 1. Pour the coconut milk and stock into a saucepan over a medium heat and stir in the laksa paste. Add the chicken strips and bring to a simmer, then reduce the heat to low and simmer for 10–15 minutes until the chicken is cooked through.

STEP 2. Stir in the tomatoes, sugar snap peas and noodles and simmer for a further 2–3 minutes. Stir in the coriander and serve immediately.

*Note: Laksa is quick and easy to prepare, especially when using ready-made laksa paste, and is eaten at all times of the day in Asia, even for breakfast. You could replace the chicken with raw peeled prawns and cook the dish in the same way.

cross the bridge noodles

Serves 4

Difficulty: Medium

Prep: 15 mins
Cook: 45–50 mins

INGREDIENTS

300 g/10½ oz dried fine egg
  noodles or rice sticks

200 g/7 oz choi sum or
  similar green vegetable

2 litres/3½ pints chicken
  stock

1-cm/½-inch piece fresh
  ginger, peeled

1–2 tsp salt

1 tsp sugar

1 boneless, skinless chicken
  breast, finely sliced
  diagonally

200 g/7 oz white fish fillet,
  thinly sliced diagonally

1 tbsp light soy sauce

STEP 1. Cook the noodles according to the packet instructions, rinse under cold running water and set aside. Bring a large saucepan of water to the boil, add the choi sum and blanch for 30 seconds. Rinse under cold running water and set aside.

STEP 2. Put the stock into a separate large saucepan and bring to the boil over a high heat, then add the ginger, 1 teaspoon of the salt and the sugar and skim the surface. Add the chicken and cook for about 4 minutes, then add the fish and simmer for a further 4 minutes, or until the fish and chicken are cooked through.

STEP 3. Add the noodles and choi sum with the soy sauce and bring back to the boil. Taste and adjust the seasoning if necessary. Serve immediately in large individual noodle bowls.

weekday meals

chicken & autumn vegetable bake

Serves 4

Difficulty: Easy

Prep: 20 mins
Cook: 40–45 mins

INGREDIENTS

3 tbsp olive oil

2 leeks, sliced

2 garlic cloves, sliced

2 large chicken breasts,
about 175 g/6 oz each,
cut into bite-sized pieces

2 sweet potatoes, peeled
and cut into chunks

2 parsnips, scrubbed and
sliced

1 red pepper, deseeded and
cut into strips

1 yellow pepper, deseeded
and cut into strips

250 g/9 oz mixed wild
mushrooms

400 g/14 oz tomatoes,
roughly chopped

300 g/10½ oz cooked white
long-grain rice

1 small bunch fresh parsley,
chopped

125 g/4½ oz mature Cheddar
cheese, grated

salt and pepper

STEP 1. Preheat the oven to 180°C/350°F/Gas Mark 4.

STEP 2. Heat the oil in a large frying pan over a medium heat, add the leeks and garlic and cook, stirring frequently, for 3–4 minutes until soft. Add the chicken and cook, stirring frequently, for 5 minutes. Add the sweet potatoes and parsnips and cook, stirring frequently, for 5 minutes, or until golden and beginning to soften. Add the peppers and mushrooms and cook, stirring frequently, for 5 minutes. Stir in the tomatoes, rice and parsley and season to taste with salt and pepper.

STEP 3. Spoon into an ovenproof dish, scatter over the cheese and bake in the preheated oven for 20–25 minutes. Serve immediately.

*Note: Scrubbing the parsnips rather than peeling them retains all the lovely flavour and nutrients that lie just under the skin. Choose small parsnips, if possible.

128

chicken, potato & leek pie

Serves 4

Difficulty: Medium

Prep: 30 mins
Cook: 1 hour 35 mins

INGREDIENTS

225 g/8 oz waxy potatoes,
  cubed

5 tbsp butter

1 skinless, boneless chicken
  breast, about 175 g/6 oz,
  cubed

1 leek, sliced

150 g/5½ oz chestnut
  mushrooms, sliced

2½ tbsp plain flour

300 ml/10 fl oz milk

1 tbsp Dijon mustard

2 tbsp chopped fresh sage

225 g/8 oz filo pastry, thawed
  if frozen

3 tbsp melted butter

salt and pepper

STEP 1. Preheat the oven to 180°C/350°F/Gas Mark 4.
Bring a saucepan of lightly salted water to the boil, add
the potato cubes, bring back to the boil and cook for
5 minutes. Drain and set aside.

STEP 2. Melt the butter in a frying pan, add the chicken
cubes and cook for 5 minutes, or until brown all over.

STEP 3. Add the leek and mushrooms and cook for
3 minutes, stirring constantly. Stir in the flour and cook
for 1 minute, stirring constantly. Gradually stir in the milk
and bring to the boil. Add the mustard, sage and potato
cubes and simmer for 10 minutes. Season to taste with
salt and pepper.

STEP 4. Meanwhile, line a deep pie dish with half of the
filo pastry. Spoon the filling into the dish and cover with a
sheet of pastry. Brush with butter and lay a second sheet
on top. Brush this sheet with butter.

STEP 5. Cut the remaining pastry into strips and fold them
on the top of the pie to create a ruffled effect. Brush the
strips with the melted butter and cook in the preheated
oven for 45 minutes, or until golden brown and crisp.
Serve hot.

classic chicken pie with cinnamon

Serves 4–6

Difficulty: Medium

Prep: 30 mins, plus cooling
Cook: 40 mins

INGREDIENTS

2–3 tbsp olive oil

100 g/3½ oz butter

3 onions, halved lengthways,
   then halved crossways and
   sliced with the grain

2 garlic cloves, chopped

2–3 tbsp blanched almonds,
   chopped

1–2 tsp ground cinnamon,
   plus extra for dusting

1 tsp ground ginger

1 tsp paprika

1 tsp ground coriander

250 g/9 oz chicken
   breast fillets, cut into
   bite-sized pieces

1 bunch fresh flat-leaf
   parsley, finely chopped

1 large bunch fresh
   coriander, finely chopped

7–8 sheets filo pastry, thawed
   if frozen

1 egg yolk, mixed with
   1 tsp water

salt and pepper

STEP 1. Preheat the oven to 200°C/400°F/Gas Mark 6. Heat the oil in a heavy-based frying pan with a knob of the butter, add the onions and cook over a medium heat, stirring frequently, for 2–3 minutes.

STEP 2. Stir in the garlic and almonds and cook for 2 minutes, stirring, then add the cinnamon, ginger, paprika and ground coriander. Add the chicken and cook gently for 3–4 minutes, or until all the liquid in the pan has evaporated. Add the parsley and fresh coriander, season to taste with salt and pepper and leave to cool.

STEP 3. Melt the remaining butter in a small saucepan. Separate the sheets of pastry and keep covered with a clean, damp tea towel while you are working. Brush a little melted butter over the base of a round ovenproof dish and cover with a sheet of pastry, allowing the sides to flop over the edge. Brush with butter and place another sheet on top. Repeat with a further two layers.

STEP 4. Spread the chicken and onion mixture on top of the pastry and fold the edges over the filling. Cover with the remaining sheets of pastry, brushing each one with butter. Tuck the overlapping edges under the pie. Brush the egg yolk mixture over the top of the pie to glaze. Bake in the preheated oven for 25 minutes, or until the pastry is puffed up and golden. Dust the top with cinnamon and serve immediately.

chicken lasagne

Serves 4–6

Difficulty: Medium

Prep: 30 mins

Cook: 1 hour 15 mins–1 hour 25 mins

INGREDIENTS

2 tbsp olive oil

1 large onion, finely chopped

500 g/1 lb 2 oz fresh
chicken mince

100 g/3½ oz smoked
pancetta, chopped

250 g/9 oz chestnut
mushrooms, chopped

100 g/3½ oz dried porcini
mushrooms, soaked

150 ml/5 fl oz dry white wine

400 g/14 oz canned chopped
tomatoes

3 tbsp chopped fresh basil
leaves

9 sheets dried lasagne

3 tbsp finely grated
Parmesan cheese

salt

WHITE SAUCE

600 ml/1 pint milk

55 g/2 oz butter

55 g/2 oz plain flour

1 bay leaf

salt and pepper

STEP 1. Preheat the oven to 190°C/375°F/Gas Mark 5. To make the white sauce, put the milk, butter, flour and bay leaf into a large saucepan and heat, whisking constantly, until smooth and thick. Season to taste with salt and pepper, then cover and set aside until needed.

STEP 2. Heat the oil in a large saucepan add the onion and fry, stirring, for 3–4 minutes. Add the chicken and pancetta and cook for 6–8 minutes. Stir in the chestnut mushrooms and porcini mushrooms and cook for a further 2–3 minutes. Add the wine and bring to the boil. Pour in the tomatoes, cover and simmer for 20 minutes. Stir in the basil.

STEP 3. Meanwhile, bring a large saucepan of lightly salted water to the boil. Add the lasagne sheets, bring back to the boil and cook according to the packet instructions. Drain well on a clean tea towel. Arrange three of the lasagne sheets in a rectangular ovenproof dish, then spoon over a third of the meat sauce.

STEP 4. Remove and discard the bay leaf from the white sauce. Spread a third of the sauce over the meat. Repeat the layers twice more, finishing with a layer of white sauce. Sprinkle with the cheese and bake in the preheated oven for 35–40 minutes until the topping is golden brown and bubbling. Serve immediately.

chicken bake

Serves 4

Difficulty: Medium

Prep: 30 mins

Cook: 1 hour 15 mins–1 hour 20 mins

INGREDIENTS

4 skinless, boneless chicken
   breasts

2 aubergines, sliced

4 tbsp plain flour

275 ml/9½ fl oz olive oil

55 g/2 oz dry breadcrumbs

1 egg

55 g/2 oz freshly grated
   Parmesan cheese

chopped fresh flat-leaf
   parsley, to garnish

salt and pepper

TOMATO SAUCE

25 g/1 oz butter

2 tbsp olive oil

1 onion, finely chopped

2 garlic cloves, finely chopped

1 celery stick, finely chopped

400 g/14 oz canned chopped
   tomatoes

2 tbsp tomato purée

6 olives, stoned and sliced

brown sugar, to taste

1 tsp dried oregano

100 ml/3½ fl oz water

salt and pepper

STEP 1. Put the chicken between two sheets of clingfilm and beat with a meat mallet until thin and even. Cut into 10-cm/4-inch long pieces and set aside. To make the sauce, melt the butter with the oil in a saucepan. Add the onion, garlic and celery and cook over a low heat, stirring occasionally, for 5 minutes until soft. Stir in the tomatoes, tomato purée, olives, sugar, oregano and water and season to taste with salt and pepper. Increase the heat to medium and bring to the boil, then reduce the heat and simmer, stirring occasionally, for 15–20 minutes until thickened.

STEP 2. Meanwhile, dip the aubergine slices in the flour to coat. Heat 5 tablespoons of the oil in a large frying pan, add the aubergine slices, in batches, and cook for 3 minutes on each side until lightly browned, adding more oil as necessary.

STEP 3. Preheat the oven to 180°C/350°F/Gas Mark 4. Spread out the breadcrumbs in a shallow dish and lightly beat the egg in a separate shallow dish. Dip the chicken first in the egg and then in the breadcrumbs to coat. Heat the remaining oil in the frying pan. Add the chicken and cook over a medium heat for 2 minutes on each side until golden. Layer the chicken and aubergine slices in an ovenproof dish, pour over the sauce and sprinkle with the cheese. Bake in the preheated oven for 20 minutes until golden. Garnish with parsley and serve immediately.

mediterranean chicken parcels

Serves 6

Difficulty: Easy
Prep: 30 mins
Cook: 30 mins

INGREDIENTS

olive oil, for brushing

6 skinless, boneless chicken breasts

250 g/9 oz mozzarella cheese, sliced

500 g/1 lb 2 oz courgettes, sliced

6 large tomatoes, sliced

1 small bunch fresh basil leaves, torn

pepper

STEP 1. Preheat the oven to 200°C/400°F/Gas Mark 6. Cut out six 25-cm/10-inch squares of foil. Lightly brush with oil and set aside until required.

STEP 2. Slash each chicken breast several times with a sharp knife, then place the cheese in the cuts.

STEP 3. Divide the courgettes and tomatoes between the foil squares and season to taste with pepper. Scatter the basil over the vegetables in each parcel.

STEP 4. Place a chicken breast on top of each pile of vegetables, then wrap in the foil to enclose the chicken and vegetables, tucking in the ends.

STEP 5. Place on a baking tray and bake in the preheated oven for about 30 minutes.

STEP 6. To serve, unwrap each foil parcel and transfer the contents to warmed serving plates.

chicken breasts with a parmesan crumb topping

Serves 4

Difficulty: Easy

Prep: 15 mins
Cook: 20 mins

INGREDIENTS

4 skinless, boneless chicken
  breasts

5 tbsp green pesto

40 g/1½ oz ciabatta
  breadcrumbs

25 g/1 oz freshly grated
  Parmesan cheese

finely grated rind of
  ½ lemon

2 tbsp olive oil

salt and pepper

roasted vine tomatoes,
  to serve

STEP 1. Preheat the oven to 220°C/425°F/Gas Mark 7. Cut a deep slash in each chicken breast to make a pocket.

STEP 2. Open out the chicken breasts and spread 1 tablespoon of the pesto in each pocket.

STEP 3. Fold the chicken flesh back over the pesto and place in an ovenproof dish.

STEP 4. Mix the remaining pesto with the breadcrumbs, cheese and lemon rind.

STEP 5. Spread the breadcrumb mixture over the chicken breasts. Season to taste with salt and pepper and drizzle with the oil.

STEP 6. Bake in the preheated oven for about 20 minutes, or until the juices run clear when a skewer is inserted into the thickest part of the meat.

STEP 7. Serve hot with roasted vine tomatoes.

chicken with tomato & cinnamon sauce

Serves 4

Difficulty: Easy

Prep: 30 mins

Cook: 1 hour 15 mins

INGREDIENTS

55 g/2 oz butter

2 tbsp olive oil

4 chicken quarters

1 onion, finely chopped

2 garlic cloves, finely chopped

1 celery stick, finely chopped

400 g/14 oz canned chopped tomatoes

2 tbsp tomato purée

1 tsp Dijon mustard

brown sugar, to taste

2 tbsp lemon juice

3 tbsp chicken stock

1 tsp dried oregano

¾ tsp ground cinnamon

salt and pepper

STEP 1. Melt the butter with the oil in a flameproof casserole. Season the chicken well with salt and pepper, add to the casserole and cook over a medium heat, turning frequently, for 8–10 minutes until evenly browned. Remove from the casserole and set aside.

STEP 2. Add the onion, garlic and celery to the casserole and cook over a low heat, stirring occasionally, for 5 minutes until soft. Stir in the tomatoes, tomato purée, mustard, sugar, lemon juice, stock, oregano and cinnamon and season to taste with salt and pepper. Increase the heat to medium and bring to the boil, then reduce the heat and simmer, stirring occasionally, for 15 minutes.

STEP 3. Return the chicken to the casserole and spoon the sauce over it. Cover and simmer, stirring occasionally, for 30 minutes until the chicken is tender and cooked through. Serve immediately.

devilled chicken

Serves 4

Difficulty: Medium

Prep: 30 mins

Cook: 2 hours 40 minutes–2 hours 50 minutes

INGREDIENTS

1 whole chicken,
  weighing 2.25 kg/5 lb

2 carrots, cut into chunks

1 celery stick, cut into
  lengths

6 black peppercorns

1 bouquet garni

pinch of salt

25 g/1 oz butter, melted

fresh thyme leaves,
  to garnish

DEVIL SAUCE

25 g/1 oz butter

2 tbsp olive oil

2 shallots, finely chopped

2 garlic cloves, finely
  chopped

1 celery stick, finely chopped

400 g/14 oz canned chopped
  tomatoes

2 tbsp tomato purée

brown sugar, to taste

3 tbsp Worcestershire sauce

1 tbsp lemon juice

2 tbsp tarragon vinegar

1 bay leaf

salt and pepper

STEP 1. Put the chicken, carrots, celery, peppercorns, bouquet garni and salt into a large saucepan and pour in enough water to cover. Bring to the boil over a high heat, then reduce the heat, cover and simmer for 1½ hours until tender and cooked through. Remove from the heat and leave to cool.

STEP 2. Meanwhile, make the sauce. Melt the butter with the oil in a saucepan. Add the shallots, garlic and celery and cook over a low heat, stirring occasionally, for 5 minutes until soft. Stir in the tomatoes, tomato purée, sugar, Worcestershire sauce, lemon juice, vinegar and bay leaf and season to taste with salt and pepper. Increase the heat to medium, bring to the boil, then reduce the heat and simmer, stirring occasionally, for 15–20 minutes until thickened.

STEP 3. Preheat the grill. Remove the chicken from the pan, strain the cooking liquid into a bowl and reserve. Remove and discard the skin, cut the chicken into eight pieces and put them into a flameproof casserole. Brush with the melted butter and cook under the preheated grill for 8 minutes on each side until evenly browned.

STEP 4. Remove and discard the bay leaf from the sauce and stir in 300 ml/10 fl oz of the reserved cooking liquid. Pour the sauce over the chicken and cook over a medium heat for 10–15 minutes until the chicken is cooked through. Garnish with thyme and serve immediately.

fried chicken with tomato & bacon sauce

Serves 4

Difficulty: Easy
Prep: 30 mins
Cook: 30 mins

INGREDIENTS

25 g/1 oz butter

2 tbsp olive oil

4 skinless, boneless chicken breasts, or 8 skinless, boneless chicken thighs

TOMATO & BACON SAUCE

25 g/1 oz butter

2 tbsp olive oil

1 large onion, finely chopped

2 garlic cloves, finely chopped

1 celery stick, finely chopped

4 bacon rashers, diced

400 g/14 oz canned chopped tomatoes

2 tbsp tomato purée

brown sugar, to taste

100 ml/3½ fl oz water

1 tbsp chopped fresh basil

1 tbsp chopped fresh parsley, plus extra to garnish

salt and pepper

STEP 1. To make the sauce, melt the butter with the oil in a large saucepan. Add the onion, garlic, celery and bacon and cook over a low heat, stirring occasionally, for 5 minutes until soft. Stir in the tomatoes, tomato purée, sugar and water and season to taste with salt and pepper. Increase the heat to medium and bring to the boil, then reduce the heat and simmer, stirring occasionally, for 15–20 minutes until thickened.

STEP 2. Meanwhile, melt the butter with the oil in a large frying pan. Add the chicken and cook over a medium-high heat for 4–5 minutes on each side until brown all over.

STEP 3. Stir the basil and parsley into the sauce. Add the chicken and spoon the sauce over it. Cover and simmer for 10–15 minutes until cooked through and tender. Garnish with parsley and serve immediately.

mexican drumsticks

Serves 4

Difficulty: Easy

Prep: 20 mins
Cook: 30–35 mins

INGREDIENTS

2 tbsp oil

8 chicken drumsticks

1 onion, finely chopped

1 tsp chilli powder

1 tsp ground coriander

400 g/14 oz canned chopped
  tomatoes

2 tbsp tomato purée

125 g/4½ oz frozen
  sweetcorn

salt and pepper

mixed pepper salad,
  to serve

STEP 1. Heat the oil in a large, heavy-based frying pan, add the chicken drumsticks and cook over a medium heat until lightly browned. Remove from the pan with a slotted spoon and set aside until needed.

STEP 2. Add the onion to the pan and cook for 3–4 minutes until soft, then stir in the chilli powder and coriander and cook for a few seconds, stirring briskly so the spices do not burn. Add the tomatoes and tomato purée and stir well to combine.

STEP 3. Return the chicken to the pan and simmer for 20 minutes until tender and cooked through. Add the sweetcorn and cook for a further 3–4 minutes. Season to taste with salt and pepper.

STEP 4. Serve hot with a mixed pepper salad.

cannelloni with chicken & ham

Serves 4

Difficulty: Medium

Prep: 20 mins
Cook: 1 hour 5 minutes–1 hour 15 minutes

INGREDIENTS

1 tbsp olive oil, plus extra for brushing

1 small onion, finely chopped

175 g/6 oz fresh chicken mince

115 g/4 oz ham, finely chopped

70 g/2½ oz cream cheese with garlic and herbs

8 dried no-precook cannelloni tubes

4 tbsp freshly grated Parmesan cheese

salt and pepper

TOMATO SAUCE

25 g/1 oz butter

2 tbsp olive oil

1 onion, finely chopped

2 garlic cloves, finely chopped

1 celery stick, finely chopped

400 g/14 oz canned chopped tomatoes

2 tbsp tomato purée

brown sugar, to taste

1 tbsp chopped fresh flat-leaf parsley

100 ml/3½ fl oz water

salt and pepper

STEP 1. To make the sauce, melt the butter with the oil in a saucepan. Add the onion, garlic and celery and cook over a low heat, stirring occasionally, for 5 minutes until soft. Stir in the tomatoes, tomato purée, sugar, parsley and water and season to taste with salt and pepper. Increase the heat to medium and bring to the boil, then reduce the heat and simmer, stirring occasionally, for 20–30 minutes until thickened.

STEP 2. Preheat the oven to 190°C/375°F/Gas Mark 5. Brush an ovenproof dish with oil. Heat the oil in a frying pan, add the onion and cook over a low heat, stirring occasionally, for 5 minutes until soft. Add the chicken and cook, stirring frequently, for a further few minutes until lightly browned. Remove the pan from the heat, stir in the ham and cream cheese and season to taste with salt and pepper.

STEP 3. Fill the cannelloni tubes with the chicken mixture and put them into the prepared dish. Pour over the sauce, sprinkle with the Parmesan cheese and bake in the preheated oven for 35–40 minutes. Serve immediately.

penne with chicken & feta

Serves 4

Difficulty: Easy

Prep: 15 mins
Cook: 35–40 mins

INGREDIENTS

2 tbsp olive oil

450 g/1 lb skinless, boneless
   chicken breasts, cut into
   thin strips

6 spring onions, chopped

225 g/8 oz feta cheese, diced

4 tbsp snipped fresh chives

450 g/1 lb dried penne

salt and pepper

STEP 1. Heat the oil in a heavy-based frying pan. Add the chicken and cook over a medium heat, stirring frequently, for 5–8 minutes, or until golden all over and cooked through. Add the spring onions and cook for 2 minutes. Stir the cheese into the pan with half the chives and season to taste with salt and pepper.

STEP 2. Meanwhile, bring a large heavy-based saucepan of lightly salted water to the boil. Add the pasta, bring back to the boil and cook for 8–10 minutes, or until tender but still firm to the bite. Drain well, then transfer to a warmed serving dish.

STEP 3. Spoon the chicken mixture onto the pasta, toss lightly and serve immediately, garnished with the remaining chives.

*Note: Feta cheese is a good ingredient to use in a pasta sauce because it keeps its shape when heated and won't disintegrate when tossed with the pasta.

chicken & mushroom tagliatelle

Serves 4

Difficulty: Medium

Prep: 20 mins, plus 30 mins soaking
Cook: 1 hour–1 hour 10 minutes

INGREDIENTS

25 g/1 oz dried shiitake
  mushrooms

350 ml/12 fl oz hot water

1 tbsp olive oil

6 bacon rashers, chopped

3 skinless, boneless chicken
  breasts, cut into strips

115 g/4 oz fresh shiitake
  mushrooms, sliced

1 small onion, finely chopped

1 tsp finely chopped fresh
  oregano or marjoram

250 ml/9 fl oz chicken stock

300 ml/10 fl oz whipping
  cream

450 g/1 lb dried tagliatelle

55 g/2 oz freshly grated
  Parmesan cheese

salt and pepper

chopped fresh flat-leaf
  parsley, to garnish

STEP 1. Put the dried mushrooms in a bowl with the hot water. Leave to soak for 30 minutes until soft. Remove, squeezing the excess water back into the bowl. Strain the liquid through a fine-meshed sieve and reserve. Slice the soaked mushrooms, discarding the stems.

STEP 2. Heat the oil in a large frying pan over a medium heat. Add the bacon and chicken, then cook for about 3 minutes. Add the dried mushrooms, fresh mushrooms, onion and oregano and cook for 5–7 minutes until soft. Pour in the stock and the mushroom liquid. Bring to the boil, stirring. Simmer briskly for about 10 minutes, stirring, until reduced. Add the cream and simmer for 5 minutes, stirring, until beginning to thicken. Season to taste with salt and pepper. Remove from the heat and set aside until needed.

STEP 3. Meanwhile, bring a large saucepan of lightly salted water to the boil. Add the pasta, bring back to the boil and cook for 8–10 minutes, or until tender but still firm to the bite. Drain and transfer to a serving dish. Pour the sauce over the pasta. Add half the cheese and mix well. Sprinkle with chopped parsley and serve with the remaining cheese.

fettuccine with chicken & onion cream sauce

Serves 4

Difficulty: Medium

Prep: 20 mins
Cook: 1 hour 15 mins–1 hour 20 mins

INGREDIENTS

1 tbsp olive oil

2 tbsp butter

1 garlic clove, very finely chopped

4 skinless, boneless chicken breasts

1 onion, finely chopped

1 chicken stock cube, crumbled

125 ml/4 fl oz water

300 ml/10 fl oz double cream

175 ml/6 fl oz milk

6 spring onions, sliced diagonally

35 g/1¼ oz freshly grated Parmesan cheese

450 g/1 lb dried fettuccine

salt and pepper

chopped fresh flat-leaf parsley, to garnish

STEP 1. Heat the oil and butter with the garlic in a large frying pan over a medium-low heat. Cook until the garlic is just beginning to colour. Add the chicken and increase the heat to medium. Cook for 4–5 minutes on each side until the juices are no longer pink. Season to taste with salt and pepper. Remove from the heat. Remove the chicken from the pan, leaving the oil in the pan. Slice the chicken diagonally into thin strips and set aside.

STEP 2. Reheat the oil in the pan. Add the onion and gently cook for 5 minutes until soft. Add the crumbled stock cube and the water. Bring to the boil, then simmer over a medium-low heat for 10 minutes. Stir in the cream, milk, spring onions and cheese. Simmer until heated through and slightly thickened.

STEP 3. Meanwhile, bring a large saucepan of lightly salted water to the boil. Add the pasta, bring back to the boil and cook for 8–10 minutes, or until tender but still firm to the bite. Drain and transfer to a warmed serving dish. Layer the chicken slices over the pasta. Pour over the sauce, garnish with parsley and serve.

penne with chicken & rocket

Serves 4

Difficulty: Medium

Prep: 30 mins
Cook: 40 mins

INGREDIENTS

25 g/1 oz butter

2 carrots, cut into thin batons

1 small onion, finely chopped

225 g/8 oz skinless, boneless
  chicken breasts, diced

225 g/8 oz mushrooms,
  quartered

125 ml/4 fl oz dry white wine

125 ml/4 fl oz chicken stock

2 garlic cloves, finely
  chopped

2 tbsp cornflour

4 tbsp water

2 tbsp single cream

125 ml/4 fl oz natural yogurt

2 tsp fresh thyme leaves,
  plus extra sprigs to garnish

115 g/4 oz rocket

350 g/12 oz dried penne

salt and pepper

STEP 1. Melt the butter in a heavy-based frying pan. Add the carrots and cook over a medium heat, stirring frequently, for 2 minutes. Add the onion, chicken, mushrooms, wine, stock and garlic and season to taste with salt and pepper. Put the cornflour and water into a bowl and mix to a smooth paste, then stir in the cream and yogurt. Stir the cornflour mixture into the pan with the thyme, cover and simmer for 5 minutes. Place the rocket on top of the chicken, but do not stir. Cover and cook for 5 minutes, or until the chicken is tender.

STEP 2. Strain the cooking liquid into a saucepan, then transfer the chicken and vegetables to a dish and keep warm. Heat the cooking liquid, whisking occasionally, for 10 minutes, or until reduced and thickened.

STEP 3. Meanwhile, bring a large heavy-based saucepan of lightly salted water to the boil. Add the pasta, bring back to the boil and cook for 8–10 minutes, or until tender but still firm to the bite. Return the chicken and vegetables to the cooking liquid and stir to coat.

STEP 4. Drain the pasta well, transfer to a warmed serving dish and spoon the chicken and vegetable mixture on top. Garnish with thyme sprigs and serve immediately.

spaghetti with parsley chicken

Serves 4

Difficulty: Easy

Prep: 20 mins
Cook: 45 mins

INGREDIENTS

1 tbsp olive oil

thinly pared rind of 1 lemon,
    cut into julienne strips

1 tsp finely chopped fresh
    ginger

1 tsp sugar

225 ml/8 fl oz chicken stock

250 g/9 oz dried spaghetti

55 g/2 oz butter

225 g/8 oz skinless, boneless
    chicken breasts, diced

1 red onion, finely chopped

leaves from 2 bunches of flat-
    leaf parsley

salt

STEP 1. Heat the oil in a heavy-based saucepan. Add the lemon rind and cook over a low heat, stirring frequently, for 5 minutes. Stir in the ginger and sugar, season to taste with salt and cook, stirring constantly, for a further 2 minutes. Pour in the stock, bring to the boil, then cook for 5 minutes, or until the liquid has reduced by half.

STEP 2. Meanwhile, bring a large saucepan of lightly salted water to the boil. Add the pasta, bring back to the boil and cook for 8–10 minutes, or until tender but still firm to the bite.

STEP 3. Melt half the butter in a frying pan. Add the chicken and onion and cook, stirring frequently, for 5 minutes, or until the chicken is lightly browned all over. Stir in the lemon and ginger mixture and cook for 1 minute. Stir in the parsley leaves and cook, stirring constantly, for a further 3 minutes.

STEP 4. Drain the pasta and transfer to a warmed serving dish, then add the remaining butter and toss well. Add the chicken sauce, toss again and serve.

fried chilli chicken

Serves 4

Difficulty: Medium

Prep: 30 mins, plus 30 mins standing
Cook: 1 hour–1 hour 5 minutes

INGREDIENTS

750 g/1 lb 10 oz chicken
  thighs

3 tbsp lemon juice

1 tsp salt, or to taste

5 large garlic cloves, roughly
  chopped

5-cm/2-inch piece fresh
  ginger, roughly chopped

1 onion, roughly chopped

2 fresh red chillies, roughly
  chopped

4 tbsp groundnut oil

1 tsp ground turmeric

½ tsp chilli powder

150 ml/5 fl oz lukewarm
  water

3–4 fresh green chillies

cooked basmati rice,
  to serve

STEP 1. Put the chicken into a non-metallic bowl and rub in the lemon juice and salt. Set aside for 30 minutes.

STEP 2. Meanwhile, put the garlic, ginger, onion and red chillies into a food processor or blender and process to a purée. Add a little water, if necessary, to help blade movement if using a blender.

STEP 3. Heat the oil in a wide, shallow non-stick saucepan over a medium-high heat. Add the chicken to the pan in two batches and cook until golden brown on all sides. Drain on kitchen paper.

STEP 4. Add the fresh spice paste to the pan with the turmeric and chilli powder and reduce the heat to medium. Cook for 5–6 minutes, stirring regularly.

STEP 5. Add the chicken and water. Bring to the boil, reduce the heat to low, cover and cook for 20 minutes. Increase the heat to medium, cover and cook for a further 8–10 minutes, stirring halfway through to ensure that the thickened sauce does not stick to the base of the pan.

STEP 6. Remove the lid and cook until the sauce is reduced to a paste-like consistency, stirring regularly to prevent the sauce sticking. Add the green chillies, cook for 2–3 minutes, remove from the heat and serve with basmati rice.

crispy-coated chicken breasts with wedges

Serves 4

Difficulty: Medium

Prep: 30 mins
Cook: 50–55 mins

INGREDIENTS

SWEET POTATO WEDGES

4 large sweet potatoes, peeled and cut into wedges

4 tbsp vegetable oil

1 tsp chilli powder

CRISPY-COATED CHICKEN

50 g/1¾ oz hazelnuts, toasted and ground

25 g/1 oz dried white or wholemeal breadcrumbs

2 tbsp grated pecorino cheese

1 tbsp chopped fresh parsley

4 skinless, boneless chicken breasts

1 egg, beaten

4 tbsp vegetable oil

salt and pepper

fresh parsley sprigs, to garnish

lemon wedges, to serve

STEP 1. Preheat the oven to 200°C/400°F/Gas Mark 6. To make the potato wedges, bring a large saucepan of water to the boil. Add the potatoes, bring back to the boil and cook for 5 minutes, then drain. Pour 2 tablespoons of the oil into a bowl and stir in the chilli powder. Add the potatoes and turn in the mixture until coated. Transfer to a baking sheet, drizzle over the remaining oil and bake in the preheated oven for 35–40 minutes, turning frequently, until golden and cooked through.

STEP 2. About 15 minutes before the end of the cooking time, put the hazelnuts, breadcrumbs, cheese and parsley into a bowl, season to taste with salt and pepper and mix to combine. Dip the chicken breasts into the egg, then the breadcrumb mixture, turning to coat.

STEP 3. Heat the oil in a frying pan. Add the chicken and cook over a medium heat for 3–4 minutes on each side until golden. Lift out and drain on kitchen paper.

STEP 4. Remove the potatoes from the oven, divide between four warmed serving plates and place a chicken breast on each plate. Garnish with parsley and serve with lemon wedges.

thai green chicken curry

Serves 4

Difficulty: Easy

Prep: 20 mins

Cook: 25–30 mins

INGREDIENTS

2 tbsp groundnut oil or sunflower oil

2 tbsp ready-made Thai green curry paste

500 g/1 lb 2 oz skinless boneless chicken breasts, cut into cubes

2 kaffir lime leaves, roughly torn

1 lemon grass stalk, finely chopped

225 ml/8 fl oz canned coconut milk

16 baby aubergines, halved

2 tbsp Thai fish sauce

fresh Thai basil sprigs and kaffir lime leaves, thinly sliced, to garnish

STEP 1. Heat the oil in a preheated wok or large, heavy-based frying pan. Add the curry paste and stir-fry briefly until all the aromas are released.

STEP 2. Add the chicken, lime leaves and lemon grass and stir-fry for 3–4 minutes until the chicken is beginning to colour. Add the coconut milk and aubergines and simmer gently for 8–10 minutes, or until tender.

STEP 3. Stir in the fish sauce and serve immediately, garnished with Thai basil sprigs and lime leaves.

*Note: This really is very quick and easy to prepare, using ready-made green curry paste. For the best results, use a good brand of coconut milk and do make the effort to find baby aubergines — they're more authentic in this dish.

easy chicken curry

Serves 4

Difficulty: Easy

Prep: 20 mins
Cook: 40–50 mins

INGREDIENTS

25 g/1 oz butter

4 tbsp olive oil

1 onion, finely chopped

2 garlic cloves, finely
 chopped

1 tbsp chopped fresh ginger

1 fresh green chilli, deseeded
 and chopped

1 celery stick, finely chopped

400 g/14 oz canned chopped
 tomatoes

2 tbsp tomato purée

brown sugar, to taste

½ tsp ground cumin

½ tsp ground coriander

½ tsp ground turmeric

¼ tsp garam masala

100 ml/3½ fl oz water

600 g/1 lb 5 oz diced chicken

150 ml/5 fl oz double cream

200 g/7 oz baby spinach

salt and pepper

warmed naan bread, to serve

STEP 1. Melt the butter with half the oil in a large saucepan over a low heat. Add the onion, garlic, ginger, chilli and celery and cook, stirring occasionally, for 5 minutes until soft. Stir in the tomatoes, tomato purée, sugar, cumin, coriander, turmeric, garam masala and water and season to taste with salt and pepper. Increase the heat to medium and bring to the boil, then reduce the heat and simmer, stirring occasionally, for 15–20 minutes until slightly reduced and thickened.

STEP 2. Meanwhile, heat the remaining oil in a frying pan. Add the chicken and cook over a medium heat, stirring frequently, for 5–7 minutes until lightly browned all over. Remove with a slotted spoon.

STEP 3. Stir the chicken and cream into the sauce and simmer for 6 minutes until the chicken is tender and cooked through. Add the spinach and cook, stirring constantly, for 2–4 minutes until wilted. Bring back to the boil, then transfer to a warmed serving dish. Serve immediately with naan bread.

chicken tikka masala

Serves 4–6

Difficulty: Easy

Prep: 30 mins
Cook: 20–25 mins

INGREDIENTS

30 g/1 oz ghee or 2 tbsp
  vegetable oil or groundnut
  oil

1 large garlic clove, finely
  chopped

1 fresh red chilli, deseeded
  and chopped

2 tsp ground cumin

2 tsp paprika

400 g/14 oz canned chopped
  tomatoes

300 ml/10 fl oz double cream

8 pieces cooked tandoori
  chicken

salt and pepper

sprigs of fresh coriander,
  to garnish

STEP 1. Heat the ghee in a large frying pan with a lid over a medium heat. Add the garlic and chilli and stir-fry for 1 minute. Stir in the cumin, paprika and salt and pepper to taste and continue stirring for about 30 seconds.

STEP 2. Stir the tomatoes and the cream into the pan. Reduce the heat to low and simmer for about 10 minutes, stirring frequently, until reduced and thickened.

STEP 3. Meanwhile, remove the bones and skin from the chicken pieces, then cut the meat into bite-sized pieces.

STEP 4. Adjust the seasoning of the sauce, if necessary. Add the chicken pieces to the pan, cover and leave to simmer for 3–5 minutes until the chicken is heated through. Garnish with coriander sprigs and serve.

chicken korma

Serves 4

Difficulty: Medium

Prep: 30 mins
Cook: 1 hour 40 mins

INGREDIENTS

1 chicken, weighing
  1.3 kg/3 lb

225 g/8 oz ghee or butter

3 onions, thinly sliced

1 garlic clove, crushed

2.5-cm/1-inch piece fresh
  ginger, grated

1 tsp mild chilli powder

1 tsp ground turmeric

1 tsp ground coriander

½ tsp ground cardamom

½ tsp ground cinnamon

½ tsp salt

1 tbsp gram flour

125 ml/4 fl oz milk

500 ml/18 fl oz double cream

fresh coriander leaves,
  to garnish

freshly cooked rice,
  to serve

STEP 1. Put the chicken into a large saucepan, add enough water to cover and bring to the boil. Reduce the heat, cover and simmer for 30 minutes. Remove from the heat, lift out the chicken and set aside to cool. Reserve 125 ml/4 fl oz of the cooking liquid. Remove and discard the skin and bones. Cut the flesh into bite-sized pieces.

STEP 2. Heat the ghee in a large saucepan over a medium heat. Add the onions and garlic and cook, stirring, for 3 minutes, or until soft. Add the ginger, chilli powder, turmeric, ground coriander, cardamom, cinnamon and salt and cook for a further 5 minutes. Add the chicken and the reserved cooking liquid and cook for 2 minutes.

STEP 3. Blend the flour with a little of the milk and add to the pan, then stir in the remaining milk. Bring to the boil, stirring, then reduce the heat, cover and simmer for 25 minutes. Stir in the cream, cover and simmer for a further 15 minutes.

STEP 4. Garnish with coriander leaves and serve with freshly cooked rice.

entertaining

roast chicken with cumin butter

Serves 4

Difficulty: Medium

Prep: 25 mins

Cook: 1 hour 25 mins–1 hour 30 mins

INGREDIENTS

100 g/3½ oz butter, softened

½ tbsp cumin seeds, lightly crushed

½ preserved lemon, finely chopped

1 large garlic clove, crushed

1 whole chicken, about 1.5 kg/3 lb 5 oz

salt and pepper

roasted vegetables, to serve

STEP 1. Preheat the oven to 220°C/425°F/Gas Mark 7. Mash together the butter, cumin seeds, preserved lemon and garlic and season to taste with salt and pepper. Using your fingers, loosen the skin on the chicken breasts and legs. Push most of the flavoured butter under the skin, moulding it to the shape of the bird. Smear any remaining butter over the skin.

STEP 2. Put the chicken into a roasting tin and cook in the preheated oven for 20 minutes. Reduce the oven temperature to 180°C/350°F/Gas Mark 4 and cook for a further 50–55 minutes until the juices run clear when a skewer is inserted into the thickest part of the meat. Transfer the chicken to a warmed serving dish, loosely cover with foil and leave to rest for 15 minutes.

STEP 3. Pour off most of the fat from the tin. Place the tin over a medium heat and cook the juices for a few minutes, stirring in all the sediment from the base of the tin, until reduced slightly. Carve the chicken into slices, then pour over the juices. Serve with roasted vegetables.

italian chicken

Serves 6

Difficulty: Medium

Prep: 35–40 mins
Cook: 2 hours–2 hours 10 mins

INGREDIENTS

1 whole chicken, about
  2.5 kg/5 lb 8 oz

f4 resh rosemary sprigs

175 g/6 oz feta cheese,
  coarsely grated

2 tbsp sun-dried tomato
  purée

60 g/2¼ oz butter, softened

1 garlic bulb

1 kg/2 lb 4 oz new potatoes,
  halved if large

1 red pepper, deseeded and
  cut into chunks

1 green pepper, deseeded
  and cut into chunks

1 yellow pepper, deseeded
  and cut into chunks

3 courgettes, thinly sliced

2 tbsp olive oil

2 tbsp plain flour

600 ml/1 pint chicken stock

salt and pepper

STEP 1. Preheat the oven to 190°C/375°F/Gas Mark 5. Carefully cut between the skin and the top of the breast meat using a small pointed knife. Slide a finger into the slit and carefully enlarge it to form a pocket. Continue until the skin is completely lifted away from both breasts and the tops of the legs.

STEP 2. Chop the leaves from 3 rosemary sprigs. Mix with the cheese, sun-dried tomato purée, butter and pepper to taste, then spoon under the skin. Put the chicken into a large roasting tin, cover with foil and cook in the preheated oven, calculating the cooking time as 20 minutes per 500 g/1 lb 2 oz, plus 20 minutes.

STEP 3. Break the garlic bulb into cloves but do not peel. Add the vegetables and garlic to the tin. After 40 minutes, drizzle with oil, tuck in the remaining rosemary and season to taste with salt and pepper. Cook for the remaining calculated time, removing the foil for the last 40 minutes to brown the chicken.

STEP 4. Transfer the chicken and vegetables to a serving platter. Spoon the fat out of the tin (it will be floating on top) and stir the flour into the remaining cooking juices. Place the tin on the hob and cook over a medium heat for 2 minutes, then gradually stir in the stock. Bring to the boil, stirring, until thickened, then season to taste with salt and pepper. Strain into a gravy boat and serve with the chicken.

coq au vin

Serves 4

Difficulty: Medium

Prep: 30 mins

Cook: 1 hour 35 mins

INGREDIENTS

55 g/2 oz butter

2 tbsp olive oil

1.8 kg/4 lb chicken pieces

115 g/4 oz rindless smoked
  bacon, cut into strips

115 g/4 oz baby onions

115 g/4 oz chestnut
  mushrooms, halved

2 garlic cloves, finely
  chopped

2 tbsp brandy

225 ml/8 fl oz red wine

300 ml/10 fl oz chicken stock

1 bouquet garni

1 bay leaf

2 tbsp plain flour

salt and pepper

STEP 1. Melt half the butter with the oil in a large, flameproof casserole. Add the chicken and cook over a medium heat, stirring, for 8–10 minutes, or until golden brown all over. Add the bacon, onions, mushrooms and garlic and stir to combine.

STEP 2. Pour in the brandy and set it alight with a match or taper. When the flames have died down, add the wine, stock, bouquet garni and bay leaf season to taste with salt and pepper. Bring to the boil, reduce the heat and simmer gently for 1 hour, or until the chicken pieces are cooked through and tender. Meanwhile, make a beurre manié by mashing the remaining butter with the flour in a small bowl.

STEP 3. Remove and discard the bouquet garni. Transfer the chicken to a large plate and keep warm. Stir the beurre manié into the casserole, a little at a time. Bring to the boil, return the chicken to the casserole and serve.

*Note: This is a classic French peasant dish and it improves with standing overnight. Use a good red wine.

chicken pepperonata

Serves 4

Difficulty: Easy

Prep: 20 mins
Cook: 45–50 mins

INGREDIENTS

8 skinless chicken thighs

2 tbsp wholemeal flour

2 tbsp olive oil

1 small onion, thinly sliced

1 garlic clove, crushed

1 large red pepper,
   deseeded and thinly sliced

1 large yellow pepper,
   deseeded and thinly sliced

1 large green pepper,
   deseeded and thinly sliced

400 g/14 oz canned chopped
   tomatoes

1 tbsp chopped fresh
   oregano, plus extra to
   garnish

salt and pepper

crusty wholemeal bread, to
   serve

STEP 1. Toss the chicken thighs in the flour, shaking off the excess.

STEP 2. Heat the oil in a wide frying pan, add the chicken and cook quickly until sealed and lightly browned, then remove from the pan.

STEP 3. Add the onion to the pan and cook over a low heat until soft. Add the garlic, red pepper, yellow pepper, green pepper, tomatoes and oregano, then bring to the boil, stirring.

STEP 4. Arrange the chicken over the vegetables, season well with salt and pepper, then cover the pan tightly and simmer for 20–25 minutes, or until the chicken is completely cooked and tender.

STEP 5. Taste and adjust the seasoning. Garnish with oregano and serve with crusty wholemeal bread.

chicken in white wine

Serves 4

Difficulty: Medium

Prep: 25 mins
Cook: 2 hours–2 hours 10 mins

INGREDIENTS

55 g/2 oz butter

2 tbsp olive oil

2 rindless, thick streaky
  bacon rashers, chopped

115 g/4 oz baby onions,
  peeled

1 garlic clove, finely chopped

1.8 kg/4 lb chicken pieces

400 ml/14 fl oz dry white
  wine

300 ml/10 fl oz chicken stock

1 bouquet garni

115 g/4 oz button
  mushrooms

25 g/1 oz plain flour

salt and pepper

fresh mixed herbs, to garnish

STEP 1. Preheat the oven to 160°C/325°F/Gas Mark 3. Melt half the butter with the oil in a flameproof casserole. Add the bacon and cook over a medium heat, stirring, for 5–10 minutes, or until golden brown. Transfer the bacon to a large plate. Add the onions and garlic to the casserole and cook over a low heat, stirring occasionally, for 10 minutes, or until golden. Transfer to the plate. Add the chicken and cook over a medium heat, stirring constantly, for 8–10 minutes, or until golden. Transfer to the plate.

STEP 2. Drain off any excess fat from the casserole. Stir in the wine and stock and bring to the boil, stirring in all the sediment from the base of the casserole. Add the bouquet garni and season to taste with salt and pepper. Return the bacon, onions and chicken to the casserole. Cover and cook in the preheated oven for 1 hour. Add the mushrooms, re-cover and cook for 15 minutes. Meanwhile, make a beurre manié by mashing the remaining butter with the flour in a small bowl.

STEP 3. Remove the casserole from the oven and set over a medium heat. Remove and discard the bouquet garni. Whisk in the beurre manié, a little at a time. Bring to the boil, stirring constantly, then serve immediately, garnished with fresh herbs.

spiced chicken stew

Serves 6

Difficulty: Medium

Prep: 30 mins

Cook: 1 hour 35 mins–1 hour 40 mins

INGREDIENTS

1.8 kg/4 lb chicken pieces

2 tbsp paprika

2 tbsp olive oil

25 g/1 oz butter

450 g/1 lb onions, chopped

2 yellow peppers, deseeded and chopped

400 g/14 oz canned chopped tomatoes

225 ml/8 fl oz dry white wine

450 ml/16 fl oz chicken stock

1 tbsp Worcestershire sauce

½ tsp hot pepper sauce

1 tbsp finely chopped fresh parsley

325 g/11½ oz canned sweetcorn kernels, drained

425 g/15 oz canned butter beans, drained and rinsed

2 tbsp plain flour

4 tbsp water

salt

fresh parsley sprigs, to garnish

STEP 1. Season the chicken pieces with salt and dust with the paprika.

STEP 2. Heat the oil and butter in a flameproof casserole or large saucepan. Add the chicken pieces and cook over a medium heat, turning, for 10–15 minutes, or until golden all over. Transfer to a plate with a slotted spoon.

STEP 3. Add the onions and yellow peppers and cook over a low heat, stirring occasionally, for 5 minutes, or until soft. Add the tomatoes, wine, stock, Worcestershire sauce, hot pepper sauce and parsley and bring to the boil, stirring. Return the chicken to the casserole, cover and simmer, stirring occasionally, for 30 minutes.

STEP 4. Add the sweetcorn and beans to the casserole, partially re-cover and simmer for a further 30 minutes. Put the flour and water into a small bowl and mix to a paste. Stir a ladleful of the cooking liquid into the paste, then stir it into the stew. Cook, stirring frequently, for a further 5 minutes. Serve immediately, garnished with parsley.

hunter's chicken

Serves 4

Difficulty: Easy

Prep: 20 mins
Cook: 1 hour 35 mins

INGREDIENTS

15 g/½ oz unsalted butter

2 tbsp olive oil

1.8 kg/4 lb skinned chicken pieces

2 red onions, sliced

2 garlic cloves, finely chopped

400 g/14 oz canned chopped tomatoes

2 tbsp chopped fresh flat-leaf parsley, plus extra to garnish

6 fresh basil leaves, torn

1 tbsp sun-dried tomato purée

150 ml/5 fl oz red wine

225 g/8 oz mushrooms, sliced

salt and pepper

STEP 1. Preheat the oven to 160°C/325°F/Gas Mark 3. Heat the butter and oil in a flameproof casserole and cook the chicken over a medium-high heat, turning frequently, for 10 minutes, or until golden all over and sealed. Using a slotted spoon, transfer to a plate.

STEP 2. Add the onions and garlic to the casserole and cook over a low heat, stirring occasionally, for 10 minutes, or until soft and golden. Add the tomatoes, herbs, sun-dried tomato purée and wine, and season to taste with salt and pepper. Bring to the boil, then return the chicken to the casserole, pushing down into the sauce.

STEP 3. Cover and cook in the preheated oven for 50 minutes. Add the mushrooms and cook for a further 10 minutes, or until the chicken is tender and the juices run clear when a skewer is inserted into the thickest part of the meat. Garnish with chopped parsley and serve.

*Note: This is a version of a traditional Italian dish that was simmered on the fire all day to feed the men after a day's hunting.

sunshine chicken

Serves 4

Difficulty: Medium

Prep: 30 mins

Cook: 55 mins

INGREDIENTS

450 g/1 lb skinless, boneless chicken

1½ tbsp plain flour

1 tbsp olive oil

1 onion, cut into wedges

2 celery sticks, sliced

150 ml/5 fl oz orange juice

300 ml/10 fl oz chicken stock

1 tbsp light soy sauce

1–2 tsp clear honey

1 tbsp grated orange rind

1 orange pepper, deseeded and chopped

225 g/8 oz courgettes, sliced into half moons

2 small corn cobs, halved, or 100 g/3½ oz baby corn

1 orange, peeled and segmented

salt and pepper

1 tbsp chopped fresh parsley, to garnish

STEP 1. Cut the chicken into bite-sized pieces. Put the flour into a large bowl and season well with salt and pepper. Toss the chicken in the flour until well coated, reserving the flour remaining in the bowl.

STEP 2. Heat the oil in a large, heavy-based frying pan, add the chicken and cook over a high heat, stirring frequently, for 5 minutes, or until golden all over and sealed. Use a slotted spoon to transfer the chicken to a plate.

STEP 3. Add the onion and celery to the pan and cook over a medium heat, stirring frequently, for 5 minutes, or until soft. Sprinkle in the reserved seasoned flour and cook, stirring constantly, for 2 minutes, then remove from the heat. Gradually stir in the orange juice, stock, soy sauce and honey, followed by the orange rind, then return to the heat and bring to the boil, stirring.

STEP 4. Return the chicken to the pan. Reduce the heat, cover and simmer, stirring occasionally, for 15 minutes. Add the orange pepper, courgettes and corn and simmer for a further 10 minutes, or until the chicken and vegetables are tender. Add the orange segments, stir well and heat through for 1 minute. Serve garnished with the parsley.

chicken with garlic

Serves 6

Difficulty: Medium

Prep: 30 mins
Cook: 1 hour 20 mins

INGREDIENTS

4 tbsp plain flour

hot or smoked sweet Spanish
paprika, to taste

1 large chicken, about
1.75 kg/3 lb 12 oz, cut into
8 pieces

4–6 tbsp olive oil

24 large garlic cloves, peeled
and halved

450 ml/15 fl oz chicken stock

4 tbsp dry white wine,
such as Rioja

1 bouquet garni

salt and pepper

fresh flat-leaf parsley and
thyme leaves, to garnish

STEP 1. Sift the flour onto a large plate and season to taste with paprika and salt and pepper. Coat the chicken pieces with the flour on both sides, shaking off the excess. Heat 4 tablespoons of the oil in a large, deep frying pan or flameproof casserole over a medium heat. Add the garlic and fry, stirring frequently, for about 2 minutes to flavour the oil. Remove the garlic with a slotted spoon and set aside to drain on kitchen paper.

STEP 2. Working in batches, add the chicken pieces to the pan skin side down, adding a little extra oil if necessary. Fry for 5 minutes until the skin is golden brown. Turn over and fry for a further 5 minutes, then transfer to a plate.

STEP 3. Pour off any excess oil. Return the garlic and chicken pieces to the pan and add the stock, wine and bouquet garni. Bring to the boil, then reduce the heat, cover and simmer for 20–25 minutes until the chicken is cooked through and tender and the garlic is very soft.

STEP 4. Transfer the chicken pieces to a serving platter and keep warm. Bring the cooking liquid to the boil and boil until reduced to about 300 ml/10 fl oz. Remove and discard the bouquet garni. Taste and adjust the seasoning, if necessary. Spoon the sauce and the garlic over the chicken. Garnish with parsley and thyme leaves.

louisiana chicken

Serves 4

Difficulty: Easy

Prep: 30 mins
Cook: 1 hour 15 mins–1 hour 20 mins

INGREDIENTS

5 tbsp sunflower oil

4 chicken pieces

55 g/2 oz plain flour

1 onion, chopped

2 celery sticks, sliced

1 green pepper, deseeded
   and chopped

2 garlic cloves, finely
   chopped

2 tsp chopped fresh thyme

2 fresh red chillies, deseeded
   and finely chopped

400 g/14 oz canned chopped
   tomatoes

300 ml/10 fl oz chicken stock

salt and pepper

chopped fresh thyme, to
   garnish

lamb's lettuce, to serve

STEP 1. Heat the oil in a large, heavy-based saucepan or flameproof casserole. Add the chicken and cook over a medium heat, stirring, for 5–10 minutes, or until golden. Transfer the chicken to a plate with a slotted spoon.

STEP 2. Stir the flour into the oil and cook over a very low heat, stirring constantly, for 15 minutes, or until light golden. Add the onion, celery and green pepper and cook, stirring constantly, for 2 minutes. Add the garlic, thyme and chillies and cook, stirring, for 1 minute.

STEP 3. Stir in the tomatoes, then gradually stir in the stock. Return the chicken pieces to the pan, cover and simmer for 45 minutes, or until the chicken is cooked through and tender. Season to taste with salt and pepper, transfer to warmed serving plates and serve immediately, garnished with a sprinkling of chopped thyme and with some lettuce on the side..

*Note: If you prefer a spicier finish, don't deseed the chillies — most of the heat is in the seeds.

194

chicken tagine

Serves 4

Difficulty: Medium

Prep: 25 mins
Cook: 30–35 mins

INGREDIENTS

1 tbsp olive oil

1 onion, cut into small
  wedges

2–4 garlic cloves, sliced

450 g/1 lb skinless, boneless
  chicken breast, diced

1 tsp ground cumin

2 cinnamon sticks,
  lightly bruised

1 tbsp wholemeal flour

225 g/8 oz aubergine,
  diced

1 red pepper, deseeded and
  chopped

85 g/3 oz button mushrooms,
  sliced

1 tbsp tomato purée

600 ml/1 pint chicken stock

280 g/10 oz canned
  chickpeas, drained and
  rinsed

55 g/2 oz ready-to-eat dried
  apricots, chopped

salt and pepper

1 tbsp chopped fresh
  coriander, to garnish

STEP 1. Heat the oil in a large saucepan over a medium heat, add the onion and garlic and cook for 3 minutes, stirring frequently. Add the chicken and cook, stirring constantly, for a further 5 minutes, or until sealed on all sides. Add the cumin and cinnamon sticks to the pan halfway through.

STEP 2. Sprinkle the flour into the pan and cook, stirring constantly, for 2 minutes. Add the aubergines, red pepper and mushrooms and cook for 2 minutes, stirring.

STEP 3. Blend the tomato purée with the stock, stir into the pan and bring to the boil. Reduce the heat and add the chickpeas and apricots. Cover and simmer for 15–20 minutes, or until the chicken is tender.

STEP 4. Season to taste with salt and pepper and serve immediately, sprinkled with chopped coriander.

spanish chicken with tomato & chocolate sauce

Serves 6

Difficulty: Easy

Prep: 20 mins
Cook: 1 hour 15 mins

INGREDIENTS

6 chicken pieces

plain flour, for dusting

4 tbsp olive oil

grated plain chocolate, to
 garnish

TOMATO & CHOCOLATE SAUCE

25 g/1 oz butter

2 tbsp olive oil

1 onion, finely chopped

2 garlic cloves, finely chopped

1 red pepper, deseeded and
 sliced

800 g/1 lb 12 oz canned
 chopped tomatoes

2 tbsp tomato purée

brown sugar, to taste

½ tsp ground nutmeg

½ tsp ground cinnamon

¼ tsp ground cloves

250 ml/9 fl oz dry white wine

70 g/2½ oz plain chocolate,
 finely chopped

salt and pepper

STEP 1. Dust the chicken with flour. Heat the oil in a large frying pan. Add the chicken, in batches if necessary, and cook over a medium heat, turning occasionally, for 8–10 minutes until brown all over. Remove from the pan and drain on kitchen paper.

STEP 2. Drain the fat from the pan and wipe out with kitchen paper. To make the sauce, melt the butter with the oil in a large saucepan. Add the onion, garlic and red pepper and cook over a low heat, stirring occasionally, for 5 minutes until soft. Stir in the tomatoes, tomato purée, sugar, nutmeg, cinnamon, cloves and wine and season to taste with salt and pepper. Increase the heat to medium and bring to the boil.

STEP 3. Return the chicken to the pan, reduce the heat, cover and simmer for 20 minutes. Remove the lid from the pan and simmer for a further 20 minutes until the chicken is cooked through and tender and the sauce has thickened. Add the chocolate and stir constantly until it has melted. Garnish with grated chocolate and serve.

chicken with tomato sauce & melted mozzarella

Serves 6

Difficulty: Medium

Prep: 20–30 mins
Cook: 55 mins–1 hour

INGREDIENTS

6 bacon rashers

25 g/1 oz butter

2 tsp chopped fresh tarragon

6 skinless, boneless chicken
  breasts, about
  175 g/6 oz each

115 g/4 oz mozzarella
  cheese, sliced

RICH TOMATO SAUCE

25 g/1 oz butter

2 tbsp olive oil

1 onion, finely chopped

2 garlic cloves, finely
  chopped

1 celery stick, finely chopped

400 g/14 oz canned chopped
  tomatoes

2 tbsp tomato purée

brown sugar, to taste

1 tsp dried oregano

100 ml/3½ fl oz water

salt and pepper

STEP 1. To make the sauce, melt the butter with the oil in a large saucepan. Add the onion, garlic and celery and cook over a low heat, stirring occasionally, for 5 minutes until soft. Stir in the tomatoes, tomato purée, sugar, oregano and water and season to taste with salt and pepper. Increase the heat to medium and bring to the boil, then reduce the heat and simmer, stirring occasionally, for 15–20 minutes until thickened.

STEP 2. Meanwhile, dry-fry the bacon in a large frying pan over a medium heat for 5 minutes. Remove from the pan and drain on kitchen paper. Add the butter to the pan and heat until melted, then stir in the tarragon, add the chicken and cook, turning occasionally, for 15–20 minutes until cooked through and tender.

STEP 3. Preheat the grill to hot. Transfer the chicken to an ovenproof dish and place a bacon rasher on top of each breast. Pour over the sauce, cover with the cheese and cook under the preheated grill for 4–5 minutes until the cheese is melted and lightly browned. Serve immediately.

chicken in tomato & almond sauce

Serves 4

Difficulty: Medium

Prep: 35–40 mins
Cook: 55 mins

INGREDIENTS

25 g/1 oz butter

2 tbsp olive oil

2 shallots, finely chopped

3 garlic cloves, finely chopped

1 celery stick, finely chopped

55 g/2 oz ground almonds

4 tbsp fresh breadcrumbs

3 tbsp chopped fresh flat-leaf parsley, plus extra to garnish

500 g/1 lb 2 oz plum tomatoes, peeled, cored and chopped

2 tbsp tomato purée

brown sugar, to taste

4 skinless, boneless chicken breasts

1 litre/1¾ pints hot chicken stock

juice of ½ orange

1 bouquet garni

6 black peppercorns

2 tbsp flaked almonds

salt and pepper

STEP 1. Melt the butter with the oil in a large saucepan. Add the shallots, garlic and celery and cook over a low heat, stirring occasionally, for 5 minutes until soft. Remove from the heat and stir in the ground almonds, breadcrumbs, parsley, tomatoes, tomato purée and sugar. Season to taste with salt and pepper. Return to the heat and cook, stirring constantly, for 5 minutes, or until thickened. Remove the pan from the heat.

STEP 2. Put the chicken into a separate large saucepan. Pour in the hot stock and orange juice, add the bouquet garni and peppercorns and bring just to the boil. Reduce the heat so that the water is barely simmering, cover and poach for 20 minutes until the chicken is cooked through and tender.

STEP 3. Transfer the chicken to a warmed serving dish and keep warm. Strain, reserving 5 tablespoons of the cooking liquid, then stir the reserved liquid into the sauce. Return to the heat and cook, stirring constantly, until thoroughly combined and heated through. Pour the sauce over the chicken and sprinkle with the flaked almonds. Garnish with parsley and serve immediately.

paella

Serves 6–8

Difficulty: Medium

Prep: 35–40 mins, plus 15 mins soaking
Cook: 50–55 mins

INGREDIENTS

16 live mussels, scrubbed and debearded

½ tsp saffron threads

2 tbsp hot water

350 g/12 oz paella rice

6 tbsp olive oil

6–8 chicken thighs, excess skin removed

140 g/5 oz chorizo, casing removed, cut into 5-mm/¼-inch slices

2 large onions, chopped

4 large garlic cloves, crushed

1 tsp paprika

100 g/3½ oz French beans, chopped

125 g/4½ oz frozen peas

1.3 litres/2¼ pints fish stock, chicken stock or vegetable stock

16 raw prawns, peeled and deveined

2 roasted red peppers, sliced

35 g/1¼ oz chopped fresh parsley, to garnish

salt and pepper

STEP 1. Discard any mussels with broken shells and any that refuse to close when tapped. Soak in lightly salted water for 10 minutes. Put the saffron and water in a cup and leave to soak for 5 minutes. Put the rice into a sieve and rinse in cold water until the water runs clear.

STEP 2. Heat 3 tablespoons of the oil in a paella pan or ovenproof casserole. Add the chicken and cook over a medium-high heat, turning frequently, for 5 minutes, or until golden. Transfer to a bowl. Add the chorizo to the pan and cook, stirring, for 1 minute, or until beginning to crisp. Add to the chicken. Heat the remaining oil in the pan and cook the onions, stirring frequently, for 2 minutes, then add the garlic and paprika and cook for a further 3 minutes, or until the onions are soft.

STEP 3. Add the drained rice, beans and peas and stir until coated in oil. Return the chicken and chorizo to the pan with any juices. Stir in the stock, saffron and its soaking liquid, and salt and pepper to taste and bring to the boil, stirring. Reduce the heat to low and simmer, uncovered, for 15 minutes, or until the rice is almost tender and most of the liquid has been absorbed.

STEP 4. Arrange the mussels, prawns and red peppers on top, then cover and simmer for a further 5 minutes, or until the prawns turn pink and the mussels open. Discard any mussels that remain closed. Garnish with the parsley and serve immediately.

chicken risotto with saffron

Serves 4

Difficulty: Medium

Prep: 10 mins
Cook: 50 mins

INGREDIENTS

125 g/4½ oz butter

900 g/2 lb skinless, boneless chicken breasts, thinly sliced

1 large onion, chopped

500 g/1 lb 2 oz risotto rice

150 ml/5 fl oz white wine

1 tsp crumbled saffron threads

1.3 litres/2¼ pints hot chicken stock

55 g/2 oz freshly grated Parmesan cheese

salt and pepper

STEP 1. Heat 55 g/2 oz of the butter in a deep saucepan. Add the chicken and onion and cook, stirring frequently, for 8 minutes, or until golden brown.

STEP 2. Add the rice and stir until coated in the butter. Cook, stirring constantly, for 2–3 minutes until translucent.

STEP 3. Add the wine and cook, stirring constantly, for 1 minute until reduced.

STEP 4. Mix the saffron with 4 tablespoons of the hot stock. Add to the rice and cook, stirring constantly, until it is absorbed.

STEP 5. Gradually add the remaining hot stock, a ladleful at a time. Add more liquid as the rice absorbs each addition. Cook, stirring, for 20 minutes, or until all the liquid is absorbed and the rice is creamy.

STEP 6. Remove from the heat and add the remaining butter. Mix well, then stir in the cheese until it melts. Season to taste with salt and pepper. Spoon the risotto into warmed serving dishes and serve immediately.

baked tapenade chicken

Serves 4

Difficulty: Easy

Prep: 15–20 mins
Cook: 25 mins

INGREDIENTS

4 skinless, boneless chicken breasts

4 tbsp green olive tapenade

8 thin slices smoked pancetta

2 garlic cloves, chopped

250 g/9 oz cherry tomatoes, halved

100 ml/3½ fl oz dry white wine

2 tbsp olive oil

8 slices ciabatta

salt and pepper

STEP 1. Preheat the oven to 220°C/425°F/Gas Mark 7. Place the chicken breasts on a board and cut three deep slashes into each.

STEP 2. Spread a tablespoon of the tapenade over each chicken breast, pushing it into the slashes with a palette knife. Wrap each chicken breast in two slices of pancetta. Place the chicken breasts in a shallow ovenproof dish and arrange the garlic and tomatoes around them. Season to taste with salt and pepper, then pour over the wine and 1 tablespoon of the oil.

STEP 3. Bake in the preheated oven for about 20 minutes until the chicken is tender and the juices run clear when a skewer is inserted into the thickest part of the meat. Loosely cover with foil and leave to stand for 5 minutes.

STEP 4. Meanwhile, preheat the grill to high. Brush the ciabatta with the remaining oil and cook under the preheated grill for 2–3 minutes, turning once, until golden. Transfer the chicken and tomatoes to warmed plates and spoon over the juices. Serve with the ciabatta.

steamed chicken with chilli & coriander butter

Serves 4

Difficulty: Medium

Prep: 30–40 mins
Cook: 25–30 mins

INGREDIENTS

55 g/2 oz butter, softened

1 fresh bird's eye chilli,
  deseeded and chopped

3 tbsp chopped fresh
  coriander

4 skinless, boneless
  chicken breasts, about
  175 g/6 oz each

400 ml/14 fl oz coconut milk

350 ml/12 fl oz chicken stock

200 g/7 oz basmati rice

salt and pepper

PICKLED VEGETABLES

1 carrot

½ cucumber

3 spring onions

2 tbsp rice vinegar

STEP 1. Cut out four 30-cm/12-inch squares of baking paper. Mix the butter with the chilli and coriander. Cut a deep slash into the side of each chicken breast to make a pocket. Spoon a quarter of the butter into each pocket and place 1 chicken breast on each square of baking paper. Season to taste with salt and pepper, then bring two opposite sides of the paper together on top, folding over to seal firmly. Twist the ends to seal.

STEP 2. Pour the coconut milk and stock into a large saucepan with a steamer top. Bring to the boil. Stir in the rice with a pinch of salt. Place the chicken parcels in the steamer top, cover and simmer for 15–18 minutes, stirring the rice once, until the rice is tender and the chicken is cooked through.

STEP 3. Meanwhile, to make the pickled vegetables, cut the carrot, cucumber and spring onions into fine matchsticks and sprinkle with the vinegar. Unwrap the chicken, reserving the juices, and cut in half diagonally. Serve the chicken over the rice, with the juices spooned over and the pickled vegetables on the side.

chicken, mushroom & cashew nut risotto

Serves 4

Difficulty: Medium

Prep: 10 mins
Cook: 1 hour

INGREDIENTS

55 g/2 oz butter

1 onion, chopped

250 g/9 oz skinless, boneless
  chicken breasts, diced

350 g/12 oz risotto rice

1 tsp ground turmeric

350 ml/12 fl oz white wine

1.3 litres/2¼ pints simmering
  chicken stock

75 g/2¾ oz chestnut
  mushrooms, sliced

50 g/1¾ oz cashew nuts,
  halved

salt and pepper

TO GARNISH

wild rocket leaves

freshly grated Parmesan
  cheese

fresh basil leaves

STEP 1. Melt the butter in a large saucepan over a medium heat. Add the onion and cook, stirring occasionally, for 5 minutes, or until soft. Add the chicken and cook, stirring frequently, for a further 5 minutes. Reduce the heat, add the rice and stir until coated in the butter. Cook, stirring constantly, for 2–3 minutes, or until the grains are translucent. Stir in the turmeric, then add the wine and cook, stirring constantly, for a further minute until reduced.

STEP 2. Gradually add the stock, a ladleful at a time. Stir constantly and add more liquid as the rice absorbs each addition. Increase the heat to medium so that the liquid bubbles. Cook for 20 minutes, or until all the liquid is absorbed and the rice is creamy. About 3 minutes before the end of the cooking time, stir in the mushrooms and cashew nuts. Season to taste with salt and pepper.

STEP 3. Remove the risotto from the heat and spoon into individual serving dishes. Sprinkle over the rocket, cheese and basil leaves and serve.

chilli chicken with chickpea mash

Serves 4

Difficulty: Medium

Prep: 20 mins, plus 30 mins marinating
Cook: 30–40 mins

INGREDIENTS

4 skinless, boneless
  chicken breasts, about
  140 g/5 oz each

1 tbsp olive oil

8 tsp harissa

salt and pepper

CHICKPEA MASH

2 tbsp olive oil

2–3 garlic cloves, crushed

400 g/14 oz canned
  chickpeas, drained
  and rinsed

4 tbsp milk

3 tbsp chopped fresh
  coriander, plus extra
  to garnish

salt and pepper

STEP 1. Make shallow cuts in each chicken breast. Place the chicken in a dish, brush with the oil and coat both sides with the harissa. Season well with salt and pepper, cover the dish with foil and marinate in the refrigerator for 30 minutes.

STEP 2. Preheat the oven to 220°C/425°F/Gas Mark 7. Transfer the chicken breasts to a roasting tin and roast in the preheated oven for about 20–30 minutes until tender and the juices run clear when a skewer is inserted into the thickest part of the meat.

STEP 3. Meanwhile, make the chickpea mash. Heat the oil in a saucepan and gently cook the garlic for 1 minute, then add the chickpeas and milk and heat through for a few minutes. Transfer to a blender or food processor and purée until smooth. Season to taste with salt and pepper and stir in the coriander.

STEP 4. To serve, slice the chicken breasts. Divide the chickpea mash between four warmed serving plates, top with a sliced chicken breast and garnish with coriander.

roasted chicken with sun-blush tomato pesto

Serves 4

Difficulty: Easy

Prep: 20 mins
Cook: 30 mins

INGREDIENTS

4 skinless, boneless
  chicken breasts, about
  200 g/7 oz each

1 tbsp olive oil

mixed salad, to serve

RED PESTO

125 g/4½ oz sun-blush
  tomatoes in oil (drained
  weight), chopped

2 garlic cloves, crushed

6 tbsp pine nuts, lightly
  toasted

150 ml/5 fl oz extra virgin
  olive oil

STEP 1. Preheat the oven to 200°C/400°F/Gas Mark 6. To make the pesto, put the tomatoes, garlic, 4 tablespoons of the pine nuts and the extra virgin olive oil into a food processor and blend to a coarse paste.

STEP 2. Arrange the chicken in a large, ovenproof dish or roasting tin. Brush with the olive oil, then put a tablespoon of the pesto on top of each. Using the back of a spoon, spread the pesto so that it covers the top of the chicken. (Store any remaining pesto in an airtight container in the refrigerator for up to 1 week.)

STEP 3. Roast the chicken in the preheated oven for 30 minutes, or until tender and the juices run clear when a skewer is inserted into the thickest part of the meat.

STEP 4. Sprinkle with the remaining pine nuts and serve with a mixed salad.

buttered chicken parcels

Serves 4

Difficulty: Medium

Prep: 30 mins, plus 10 mins cooling
Cook: 40 mins

INGREDIENTS

4 tbsp butter

4 shallots, finely chopped

300 g/10½ oz frozen spinach, thawed

450 g/1 lb blue cheese, such as Stilton, crumbled

1 egg, lightly beaten

1 tbsp snipped fresh chives

1 tbsp chopped fresh oregano

4 skinless, boneless chicken breasts

8 slices Parma ham

salt and pepper

baby spinach leaves, to serve

fresh chives, to garnish

STEP 1. Melt 2 tablespoons of the butter in a frying pan over a medium heat. Add the shallots and cook, stirring, for 4 minutes. Remove from the heat and leave to cool for 10 minutes.

STEP 2. Preheat the oven to 180°C/350°F/Gas Mark 4. Squeeze out as much moisture from the thawed spinach as possible and put it into a large bowl. Add the shallots, cheese, egg, herbs and salt and pepper to taste and mix well together.

STEP 3. Halve each chicken breast then place each piece between two sheets of clingfilm and pound gently with a meat mallet to flatten to an even thickness. Spoon some cheese mixture into the centre of each piece, then roll it up. Wrap each roll in a slice of ham and secure with a cocktail stick. Transfer to a roasting dish, dot with the remaining butter and bake in the preheated oven for 30 minutes until golden.

STEP 4. Divide the baby spinach leaves between four serving plates. Remove the chicken from the oven and place 2 chicken rolls on each plate. Garnish with fresh chives and serve.

chicken & spicy tomato sauce parcels

Serves 4

Difficulty: Medium

Prep: 30 mins
Cook: 1 hour–1 hour 20 mins

INGREDIENTS

4 chicken breasts,
  about 175 g/6 oz each

4 fresh tarragon sprigs

SPICY TOMATO SAUCE

25 g/1 oz butter

2 tbsp olive oil

1 onion, finely chopped

2 garlic cloves, finely
  chopped

1 celery stick, finely chopped

2 orange peppers, deseeded
  and chopped

400 g/14 oz canned chopped
  tomatoes

2 tbsp sun-dried tomato
  purée

brown sugar, to taste

1 tbsp paprika

1 tsp chilli powder

1 tsp dried thyme

100 ml/3½ fl oz water

salt and pepper

STEP 1. To make the sauce, melt the butter with the oil in a saucepan. Add the onion, garlic, celery and orange peppers and cook over a low heat, stirring occasionally, for 5 minutes until soft. Stir in the tomatoes, sun-dried tomato purée, sugar, paprika, chilli powder, thyme and water and season to taste with salt and pepper. Increase the heat to medium and bring to the boil. Reduce the heat and simmer, stirring occasionally, for 15–20 minutes until thickened.

STEP 2. Meanwhile, preheat the oven to 190°C/375°F/ Gas Mark 5. Cut out four 30-cm/12-inch squares of greaseproof paper and place one chicken breast on each square.

STEP 3. Divide the sauce between the chicken breasts and top each with a tarragon sprig. Fold the paper over fairly loosely and double-fold the edges to seal. Put the parcels on a baking sheet and bake in the preheated oven for 35–40 minutes until the chicken is cooked through and tender. Serve immediately.